How to Pass
the CPA Exam

How to Pass the CPA Exam

THE IPASSTHECPAEXAM.COM GUIDE FOR INTERNATIONAL CANDIDATES

Stephanie Ng

WILEY

Other Wiley Editorial Offices
John Wiley & Sons, 111 River Street, Hoboken, NJ 07030, USA
John Wiley & Sons, The Atrium, Southern Gate, Chichester, West Sussex,
    P019 8SQ, United Kingdom
John Wiley & Sons (Canada) Ltd., 5353 Dundas Street West, Suite 400, Toronto,
    Ontario, M9B 6HB, Canada
John Wiley & Sons Australia Ltd., 42 McDougall Street, Milton, Queensland 4064,
    Australia
Wiley-VCH, Boschstrasse 12, D-69469 Weinheim, Germany

Library of Congress Cataloging-in-Publication Data

ISBN 9781118613221 (Paperback)
ISBN 9781118613238 (ePDF)
ISBN 9781118613245 (Mobi)
ISBN 9781118613252 (ePub)

Typeset in 11/13 pt. ITC New Baskerville Std Roman by Aptara India
Printed in Singapore by COS Printers Pte Ltd.

10 9 8 7 6 5 4 3 2 1

To my parents, and Jane, John, Megan, and Max

Contents

Chapter 13   Business Environment and Concepts (BEC)   193

Introduction

Dear Aspiring CPAs,

I am Stephanie and I have been running a popular CPA exam preparation site called IPassTheCPAExam.com since January 2010.

I originally set up the site to help candidates pick the most suitable CPA review course, but quickly realized that my readers were looking for something else.

They could not even get past the application. They were highly educated and successful accountants in their respective countries, but somehow, the U.S.-centric system made things very difficult.

I Understand the Frustration

Why? Because I have been there. I was an international candidate myself and spent countless hours of research to come up with a way that I thought would work, but it turned out that a new law had passed and I was back to square one.

Five weeks later when I figured out another path that looked workable for me, it was a hassle to go through the application process, such as getting the transcripts evaluated by what is known as the *foreign credential evaluation agencies*, and the nightmare of missing deadlines here and there . . .

I burned out before the studying began.

But I was determined to get it done—and, in fact, once I got approved for the exam, I studied hard, took the four parts in one go and passed the four sections of the exam on my first attempt (FAR: 92, REG: 84, AUD: 88, BEC: 87).

It Is Mission "Possible"

The CPA exam requirements are getting stricter since I became a CPA, but every year more than 10,000 international candidates go through the maze and get approved to sit for the exam.

If they can do it, I am sure you can, too.

How I Can Be Helpful

I have been answering readers' questions through my site for the past three years, and I am thankful for all the email, notes, blessings, gifts (I got a gift mailed to me from Pakistan) . . . but the best part is to hear the success stories from my readers.

> Hi Stephanie, I passed BEC in Jan with an 80, REG in April with a 91, and FAR in August with another 91, I scheduled AUD in 10/18, just wait for my good news! ... and don't forget: CPA Exam is passable! Thanks for my family and all my friends to keep me running!
>
> **—Yan Tan**

(Yan passed AUD with yet another 91 in October.)

This book is an extension of what is offered on my website. You can find tips on every single step, pitfalls that you should avoid during the application process, what to expect along the way, as well as a new section on how to study for the CPA exam for candidates with an international background.

Throughout the book you can read stories of my readers in different parts of the CPA journey, from those contemplating whether to make the jump, those in the middle of studying, to those who have passed the exam and got their licenses. I hope these personal accounts make this book a more enjoyable read.

You will also find three icons that highlight the text in the form of definitions, notes, and tips.

The definition box is used to introduce the acronyms that you will come across in your CPA journey.

Note

The note box draws attention to important reminders.

TIP

The tip box is my special place for words of advice.

How You Can Be Helpful

I understand that many of my readers are highly educated and experienced finance professionals in your respective countries. Being a CPA is not only about getting a better job and making more money; it is also about how you can make good use of your expertise to give back to the community.

For me, I am going to donate all the royalties from this book to two worthy causes:

1. New Sight Eye Care: A U.K.-registered charity founded by a dear friend and her husband, Joyce and Henri Samoutou. They, together with their three young children, are now in the Republic of Congo establishing the first eye surgical center. Follow their amazing work on their website at www .newsightcongo.com.
2. The other charity will be nominated and voted on by my readers. Get the latest update on my website at http:// ipassthecpaexam.com.

1

Why CPA?

First of all, I applaud your decision to take on this difficult challenge—to study for and pass the Certified Public Accountant (CPA) exam.

Everyone has a reason to become a CPA. Some aspire to become a Big 4 partner, some strive to earn recognition from peers and colleagues, while others want to enhance their credentials, or simply get a secure job that is well paid with a decent work-life balance.

Whatever your reasons might be, I can assure you that passing the CPA exam is going to be one of the most celebrated moments in your life.

What Is CPA?

CPA stands for Certified Public Accountant in the United States. It is a designation granted to individuals who pass the Uniform CPA Examination and have met the educational and working experience requirements.

In most parts of the United States, only licensed U.S. CPAs can sign audit opinions on financial statements. This statutory right differentiates U.S. CPAs from Chartered Accountants and CPAs from other countries, as well as professional designations such as Chartered Financial Analyst (CFA), Certified Management Accountants (CMA), and Certified Internal Auditor (CIA).

Unlike some other professional accounting certifications such as Association of Chartered Certified Accountants (ACCA), CPA does not have a syllabus for which candidates can sign up, take the course-work, and expect to obtain the designation on completion of the coursework.

Instead, candidates must find a way to meet the educational requirements to become eligible for the exam. We cover the educational requirements extensively in Chapter 3, "How to Get Qualified."

Five Reasons to Become a CPA

The U.S. CPA exam is considered to be one of the most challenging with a low passing rate, yet tens of thousands of candidates jump in and take the challenge every year. Why?

Increasing Demand

After the recent corporate scandals and failures, governments and the business communities have stepped in to scrutinize the corporation, pouring considerable resources to hire and train accounting professionals.

The Sarbanes-Oxley Act is believed to have increased the demand for accountants and CPAs by double-digit percentage points. The U.S. Bureau of Labor Statistics predicts that the number of jobs for accountants and auditors "is expected to grow by 22 percent between 2008 and 2018, which is much faster than the average for all occupations."

The constant demand for CPAs makes this an ideal profession for those looking for a stable and rewarding job.

> Hi Stephanie, I am a Psychology major who just graduated from college. Starting from junior year, I decided I want to become a CPA. I wanted to be able to provide my family with financial stability after seeing the stress my family went through when my mom passed away following my dad's unemployment during my sophomore year. I wasn't able to get into the accounting minor at my school but I took an equivalent amount of accounting classes and I enjoyed them. Indeed, the knowledge I gained is very practical and I found the learning process very rewarding.
>
> Right now, I am finishing up my last few online classes and getting ready to take the CPA exam.
>
> —Ying

Decreasing Supply

An intriguing national survey by the American Institute of Certified Public Accountants (AICPA) shows that 75 percent of its members are retiring in 10 years. The situation in major financial hubs is equally acute: More than 50 percent of the practitioners at the New York Society of CPA are more than 50 years old. Even in academia, the supply of accounting professors is getting tight: The average age of the accounting faculty is 55; the most common age is 63.

It takes 10 to 15 years to reach the senior positions in public, governmental, and corporate accounting, so this is the time to jump in and catch this golden opportunity.

The American Institute of Certified Public Accountants (AICPA)

The AICPA is the national professional organization for CPAs in the United States, and one of the oldest and largest accounting bodies in the world. The institute sets the U.S. auditing standards and ethical standards for the profession. It is also one of the major stakeholders in the design and administration of the Uniform CPA Examination.

The Value of Getting Recognized

Besides the demand-supply imbalance, becoming a CPA is a personal achievement. Your family, friends, and business partners will be proud of you with this globally recognized qualification.

Becoming a CPA is also a demonstrated commitment to the accounting industry. Accounting firms and companies recognize professionals who put in the investment of time, money, and effort to achieve this goal. You will get the reward when it comes to recruiting and promotion.

> Hello Stephanie. Merry Christmas! Well, almost. :) I'm writing to you because I have decided that I want to embark on this long and grueling journey towards my CPA license. I live in California, and graduated two and a half years ago. I have been working in private accounting, but feel I need my CPA license to help me move up and make more money. I feel that obtaining my CPA license will help open new opportunities or make me qualified for better paying positions.
>
> —Edgar De La Torre

At the same time, getting the CPA designation could be a matter of survival. I got many emails from readers asking for help to pass the CPA exam as soon as possible, because they had received an ultimatum from the management to get it done. Most of these readers are seasoned finance professionals with many years of practical experience; yet for one reason or another, they procrastinate until it becomes almost too late. Learn from my readers' experience and take the exam as soon as you can.

The Door to Career Change or More Interesting Career Paths

Accounting is much more than bookkeeping and auditing. There are many interesting niches once you reach a level of expertise. Forensic accounting is an exciting field. Finance and risk management careers within biotechnology and environmental engineering are options with great potential. As the economy recovers, your CPA designation will be a valuable asset when new opportunities emerge in promising industries.

If you are looking for career change, the CPA designation can help you get into accounting even though you have no prior experience.

> Hi Stephanie, my name is Donna, and I am a mere eight weeks away from completing my Master's of Science Degree in Accounting. I actually never really thought I would be interested in accounting. I obtained my Bachelor's Degree in Elementary Education way back when and taught for a few years. My husband moved around for his job (with me in tow), and after our first move I never got back into teaching. I've been in administrative roles for the last fifteen years and ended up doing some financial work in city government. I decided to utilize the city's educational assistance program to pursue my Master's Degree and decided that accounting seemed interesting (go figure . . . I usually get blank stares or comments like "Wow . . . better you than me. . . . I could never be an accountant").
>
> While I'm not certain where my hat will hang after I get my degree, I do know that the sky is the limit if I am able to get my CPA license. I'll be 44 this November, so I am anxious to get on the career ladder. With that being the case, my goal is to have all four sections of the exam passed successfully by the end of 2013.
>
> —Donna

The Route to Financial Freedom

The salary range of accountants depends on education, geography, and market condition among other factors. In general, however, CPAs can expect to earn up to 10 percent more than their peers without the professional designation. If you take into account the cumulative effect as well as the potential for CPAs to get more frequent promotions, the difference can be substantial over the lifetime of your career.

You may not become a millionaire strictly as a CPA, but you will likely pay off the mortgage, retire early, and enjoy life earlier with the help of this designation.

Five More Reasons to Become a CPA for International Candidates

As an international candidate, you may have an even greater desire to obtain the U.S. CPA designation.

It Could Be Easier Than the Local CPA Exam

It may be hard to believe, but in some parts of the world, the professional accounting examination is even tougher to pass.

In China, for example, the equivalent exam administered by the Chinese Institute of Certified Public Accountants (CICPA) has a passing rate of well below 20 percent. The exam comprises seven papers with exam topics constantly changing as the local accounting and auditing standards converge with the international standards. In comparison, the U.S. version is considerably more lenient with passing rates around 50 percent.

It is interesting to note that with the growing Chinese economy, the demand for accountants is higher than in the United States: There are currently 180,000 CICPA members but the institute aims to increase this number by almost 40 percent to 250,000 by 2015.

With this extreme demand-supply imbalance, it is logical for Chinese accountants to take the U.S. CPA exam for higher success rates and speedier processes, as long as their employers recognize non-Chinese qualifications. These U.S. CPA–qualified accountants in China are in high demand in international accounting firms and multinational corporations.

It Could Take Less Time to Become a CPA

The U.S. CPA exam consists of four sections totaling 14 hours, involving multiple-choice questions, task-based simulations, and written communications. Candidates can take the sections separately or in one go. They can also sit for the exam any time during the testing windows, which are offered in the first two months of each quarter.

In other parts of the world, the equivalent professional accounting exam often consists of several papers with long calculations and essays. Each paper is offered once or twice a year. Because of the different arrangements, a U.S. CPA candidate can technically complete the exam within a few months, while the non-U.S. counterparts have no choice but to tackle each paper one at a time.

If you want to become a CPA on a fast track, this is a great reason for you to get started.

It Allows More Flexibility

As you embark on the CPA journey, you will appreciate the flexibility offered by this exam when compared to its overseas counterparts.

First of all, the exam is 100 percent computerized, which enables low-cost delivery of the exam in a more customized and user-friendly format. By scheduling the exam on any Monday to Friday (even Saturday and Sunday for some sites) during the test windows, you can set your own pace and take the exam at a time convenient for you.

The computerized format has led to the proliferation of practice test questions offered on computers. Guided review courses are available with full offerings of videos, lecture notes, and flash cards on computer and mobile devices.

The test preparation software often comes with a study planner and diagnostics to help schedule and analyze your study process in a systematic manner. This makes self-study much easier, more efficient, and more effective.

Candidates outside the United States used to have little choice when it came to CPA review courses. Nowadays, the availability of online self-study courses has created the same level playing field. With dedication and hard work, international candidates have an equal chance to successfully pass the CPA exam.

It Could Increase Your Job Mobility

Many readers of my website are chartered accountants and their memberships span many accounting professional organizations. When they realize that these qualifications cannot be fully recognized in other parts of the world and especially in the United States, they find the need to take the U.S. CPA exam.

I also have readers who are university students with the aspiration to go abroad and work in a foreign country. They have not decided on the destination but after recognizing the global acceptance of the U.S. CPA designation, they are determined to focus their efforts on the CPA exam.

The U.S. CPA Exam Is Going International

The greatest news is that the AICPA and the National Association of State Boards of Accountancy (NASBA) want you to join! The stakeholders of the CPA exam spent two years studying the international exam delivery program. In August 2011, the first international sites were open in Japan, Bahrain, Kuwait, Lebanon, and the United Arab Emirates, followed by another site in Brazil in February 2012.

U.S. citizens living abroad and citizens of the above countries can take advantage of these international testing locations. Long-term residents of Egypt, Jordan, Lebanon, Oman, Qatar, Saudi Arabia, UAE, and Yemen can take the exam in one of the Middle Eastern locations. Long-term residents of Argentina, Colombia, and Venezuela can take the exam in Brazil.

Candidates should be aware of the restrictions involved (discussed in Chapter 3) but all in all this is an excellent sign that international candidates are welcome to join the community.

National Association of State Boards of Accountancy (NASBA)

NASBA is an association dedicated to serving the fifty-five State Boards of Accountancy. NASBA is another major stakeholder in the administration of the Uniform CPA Examination.

What Are You Waiting For?

This is the best time to make up your mind and take up the challenge! I guide you on how to achieve this goal in the most efficient and cost-effective way in later chapters.

What Is the CPA Exam?

In order to become a CPA in the United States, you need to fulfill the "Three Es" requirements: Education, Examination, and Experience. This chapter focuses on the second step, the Uniform CPA Examination. We discuss in length the educational and experience requirements in the next chapter.

Exam Coverage

Here are frequently asked questions on the coverage, format, and passing rate of the CPA exam.

What Does the Uniform CPA Exam Cover?

The exam is comprehensive, covering all accounting concepts and applications in financial accounting and auditing, together with related fields such as economics, business law, business ethics, internal control, financial management, risk management, information systems, regulations, and taxation.

There are four sections in the exam:

1. Audit and Attestation (AUD)—four hours
2. Financial Accounting and Reporting (FAR)—four hours
3. Regulation (REG)—three hours
4. Business Environment and Concepts (BEC)—three hours

We review the topics and study tips for each session in later chapters.

What Is the Exam Format?

The CPA exam is fully computerized. For FAR, AUD, and REG, the section consists of:

- Three testlets (i.e., groups) of 24 to 30 multiple-choice questions.
- One testlet of task-based simulation questions with six to seven questions, or three questions on written communications.

Multiple-Choice Questions Multiple-choice questions are graded positively in this exam. In other words, there is no penalty for incorrect answers. This has an implication on the test-taking strategy and we go over this in the second half of this book.

Task-Based Simulation Questions Also known as the *simulations*, they are "condensed case studies" to test whether candidates understand the selected concept in-depth and are able to apply the concepts in the business environment. They are also meant to assess the candidates' ability to research effectively.

Prior to 2011, there was a written communications tab within the simulation questions, which represented 10 percent of the total score. The rest of the simulations represented 20 percent. Effective January 2011, there is no written communications in FAR, AUD, and REG but you will find three written communication tasks in BEC.

To really understand how simulations work, you have to work on the practice questions online and get used to the format. You can also learn more about this exam format in Chapter 8, "How to Overcome the Fear of Task-Based Simulations."

Written Communication Tasks Candidates are asked to write a memo, letter to the client, or other types of business writing that a junior CPA is expected to perform in everyday work. You are graded on relevance, conciseness, and proper use of English instead of the technical accuracy of the content.

What Is the CPA Exam Passing Rate?

Each section is slightly different, but the overall CPA exam pass rate in 2012 was 49.0 percent. Although this is not an encouraging

Note

If English is not your first language, you may want to read Chapter 9, "How to Ace the Written Communication Tasks," on how to get comfortable with business writing for the purpose of the CPA exam.

statistic, you can greatly improve your odds by planning and studying for the exam the right way, which is the focus in the second half of this book.

Exam Schedule and Location

Here are the questions on when and where you can take the exam.

When Does the Exam Take Place?

You can take the exam anytime during the "testing window," which is the first 60 days of each calendar quarter. The testing window is the same for both U.S. and international testing locations effective January 1, 2013.

When Is the Deadline?

There is no deadline because the testing date is not fixed. However, international candidates should start the application process around four to six months before the desired test date. Extra time is required because of the additional steps in the application process for international candidates. We go over this in Chapter 3, "How to Get Qualified," and Chapter 4, "Getting Ready."

After completing a successful application, you receive the "Notice to Schedule," or NTS. This is the admission ticket that allows you to schedule the exam anytime within six months for most states, and within 9 to 12 months for a few others.

Where Can I Take the Exam?

You can sit for the exam in the Prometric centers throughout the United States and in the international exam sites in Japan, Bahrain, Kuwait, Lebanon, the United Arab Emirates, and Brazil.

Note that the international exam sites are restricted for U.S. and local citizens as well as local long-term residents. For example, a Taiwan citizen cannot take the CPA exam in Japan even though it is the most convenient location. A U.S. citizen working in Taiwan is eligible to take the exam in Japan.

Exceptions are long-term residents of Egypt, Jordan, Lebanon, Oman, Qatar, Saudi Arabia, UAE, and Yemen; they may take the exam in one of the Middle Eastern locations. Long-term residents of Argentina, Colombia, and Venezuela can schedule their exams in Brazil.

Where Can I Get the Application Form?

The application process is complicated for international candidates. There is no centralized agency to administer the application in the United States. Instead, the boards of accountancy in each of the 50 states and five territories are responsible for establishing the eligibility requirements and granting the CPA license.

You need to select a state and fulfill this particular state's requirements in order to sit for the exam. We go over the steps in detail in Chapter 3.

Can I Register in One State and Physically Sit for the Exam in Another?

Yes. For example, you can register in Colorado but physically take the exam in California where your relatives live.

For candidates from East Asia and Southeast Asia, taking the exam in Guam is the most logical choice. Note that there is a surcharge of US$110 per exam section in Guam if candidates do not register the exam through Guam.

Exam Qualifications

Here are the questions on the eligibility and possible exemptions for the exam.

I Did Not Study in the United States. Can I Qualify?

Yes, but there is an additional step in the application process. For education obtained outside the United States, you need to get your transcripts evaluated by one of the foreign credential evaluation agencies.

The list of approved agencies can be found in the CPA exam application form. You can look up the information on the National

Association of State Boards of Accountancy (NASBA) website at www
.nasba.org/exams/.

I Am a Chartered Accountant. Can I Take the CPA Exam?

In the old days, Chartered Accountants (CA) or Association of Chartered Certified Accountants (ACCA) holders could use their certificates to get qualified for the U.S. CPA exam. Since 2012, state boards
have stopped considering professional designations as equivalent to
a four-year bachelor's degree, and therefore whether you are a CA
has become irrelevant. Although a few states may count some related
coursework toward the educational requirements, you must have a
four-year bachelor's degree (or a three-year bachelor's degree and a
two-year master's degree) to become eligible for the exam.

What Are the Exemptions Available for the CPA Exam?

Only the statutory accounting bodies from the following countries
that have entered into mutual recognition agreements (MRA) with
the International Qualifications Appraisal Board (IQAB), which represents the U.S. state boards of accountancy, can get certain exemptions:

- Australia (CA only)
- Canada (CA only)
- Hong Kong
- Ireland
- Mexico
- New Zealand

Members of these institutes can take a shorter exam known as
the International Qualification Exam (IQEX) to get the license.
There are more discussions on IQEX in Chapter 3.

I Graduated from the Top University in My Country. Does It Make a Difference?

It does not make any difference, and the same applies to U.S. domestic
candidates. As long as the school you attended is regionally accredited and the candidate obtains a valid transcript on graduation, the
degree and the credit hours will be counted toward the educational
requirements. If your school is not regionally accredited, you have to
go through the foreign credential evaluation agencies.

Which Is the Best State to Register for International Candidates?

This depends largely on your educational background and how you would like to fulfill the working experience requirement. We go through the selection process in Chapter 3.

Exam-Taking Strategy

Here are the questions on how to schedule the four exam sections and how to prepare for the exam.

Can I Take Each Section One at a Time, or Several at the Same Time?

You can take one or multiple sections at any time during the testing window and in any sequence. Also, you do not need to pass a section in order to move on to the next. The only restriction is that you cannot take each section more than once within the same testing window.

For example, you cannot schedule the FAR exam in July and August of the same year (both in the same testing window of the third quarter), but you can schedule the FAR exam in July (third quarter) and November (fourth quarter). In practice, you should wait for the first FAR result before scheduling the next FAR exam.

TIP

If you need to travel to the United States to sit for the exam, I highly recommend that you take several sections in one go to save travel and accommodation cost.

Which Exam Section Should I Start First?

It depends on your area of expertise, but in general I recommend you tackle the section that takes the most time to study. For the vast majority of candidates, this would mean FAR. AUD is closely related to FAR and therefore it makes sense to take these two sections within a short period of time.

Unless you are an experienced tax professional, REG will likely be the most difficult section because it deals with U.S. taxation. BEC is the shortest section and you can schedule this section during the busiest time of the year.

We have a more extensive discussion on the sequence of the exam in Chapter 5, "Creating a Study Plan."

Is There a Time Limit to Complete the Four Sections of the Exam?

Yes. You have to complete the four sections of the exam within 18 months, counting from the time you pass the first section. Otherwise, you need to retake the sections that you passed before the 18-month period.

For example, if a candidate passes FAR on January 1, 2013, AUD on February 17, 2013, and BEC on August 23, 2013, but fails to pass REG before July 1, 2014 (i.e., 18 months after passing of FAR), then he will have to retake FAR after July 1, 2014.

If he successfully passes FAR again and REG before August 17, 2014 (i.e., 18 months after passing AUD), then he will not need to retake AUD because he would have completed all four sections of the exam within 18 months.

I recommend that candidates aim to complete the four sections within 12 months and use the remaining six months as the buffer for unplanned family/work commitments and possible retake of a few sections.

Do I Need Specific Skills for Taking the Computerized Exam?

Yes and no. The exam does require candidates to know how to perform basic calculation on spreadsheets or an onscreen calculator, and type up a few paragraphs on the computer. Basically, if you are somewhat familiar with word processors and spreadsheets, you are well prepared in this regard.

I would strongly encourage that you get familiar with the working of the spreadsheet to save time in the task-based simulation section. We expand on this point in Chapter 7, "Study Tips and Exam-Taking Strategies."

The Uniform CPA Exam website provides a tutorial and sample test for you to try out the functions, but I highly recommend that you get a CPA test preparation software so you can keep practicing at home.

How Do I Prepare for the Exam?

You need to get familiar with the exam topics as well as the format of the exam. Although it is not necessary to sign up for exam review courses, the success rate of those who do are much higher than that of the average (49.0 percent in 2012). Many top CPA review courses boast an impressive rate of more than 85 percent among their students.

Can You Suggest a CPA Review Course?

The study tips in the second half of this book is based on the *Wiley CPA Exam Review* and *Wiley Focused Notes*. If you prefer a more guided approach, there are a number of CPA review courses that provide professors teaching on videos, online CPA exam planners, lecture notes, and test preparation software.

We discuss how you can choose the most suitable review course in Chapter 7.

Exam Design and Navigation

Here are the questions on what you can expect to see in the computerized exam and the grading system.

In This Computerized Exam, Can I Go Back and Revise the Answers?

Within each testlet or simulation, you are allowed to jump around or go back to make revisions. However, once a testlet or simulation is completed and you have moved on to the next one, it is impossible to go back. It is therefore very important that you get familiar with the layout and format before the actual exam.

Is the Exam Adaptive?

Yes. Being adaptive means that the exam can get progressively more difficult depending on the candidates' performance on the previous testlet. For example, if you do well on the first testlet, your second set will be more difficult; otherwise, the level of difficulty stays the same. Multiple-choice questions are adaptive but task-based simulation questions are not.

If My Second and Third Testlets Look Really Easy, Should I Worry?

Yes, I am afraid so, because most likely you get stuck in the "medium-level" testlet because you did not answer enough questions correctly in the first and/or second testlets. The reason to worry is that the questions on these medium-level testlets are assigned a lower score than those in the difficult level, which means that you still get a lower score even if you answer the majority of the medium-level ones correctly.

How Can I Tell If the Testlet Is Easy or Difficult?

The first testlet is always at the medium level, and that is what I mean by "easy." It is quite obvious when you progress to the difficult testlets because the way the questions are framed is more complicated and wordy, and you may have several answers that seem to be right; that is, you have to think hard for the best answer.

Having said that, some candidates never experience this increase in difficulty and manage to pass with an excellent score.

With the Adaptive Model, Does It Mean the CPA Candidates Are Taking Different Exams?

Yes, the exams are different but equivalent. CPA Examination Services states that the test assembly method and expert reviews ensure that all tests meet content specifications, that is, there is a system in place to ensure that each candidate is being assessed correctly and fairly.

What Is the Passing Score? Is the Exam Scored on a Curve?

Passing score is 75, on a 0 to 99 scale. A second review is performed for candidates with grades just below 75.

Technically speaking, the CPA exam is not curved because every candidate's score is independent of other candidates' examination results. My interpretation is that although there is not a curve and that the examiners do not subjectively manipulate the test and passing rate, the scoring system has an inherent curve built into it. It means that if you get half the questions wrong, as may well be the case, you may still pass because the difficult questions get more weight.

The bottom line is not to worry too much about the scoring system. In every testing window half of the candidates pass and half do not. Your focus is to make sure you get into the first half.

I Heard There Is a Diagnostic Report, but I Never Got It. Why?

The diagnostic report is sent only to those who failed the exam. It shows the weak areas and how candidates can improve in their next attempt. We discuss the diagnostic report in more detail in Chapter 14, "What If I Fail?"

After the Exam

Here are the questions on the steps after passing the exam.

When and How Do I Get the Results?

The quickest way to find out your score is to check the results online. The scores are released in three batches: day 1 to day 20 of the testing window, day 21 to day 45 of the testing window, and day 46 to the close of testing window. The score is released 6 to 11 business days after day 20, day 45, and last day of the testing window respectively. This means that you can get the results as early as 6 business days and as late as 31 days depending on which day you take the test.

You can get the latest score release timetable at http://ipassthe cpaexam.com/aicpa-score-release/.

Do I Get My License Immediately after Passing the CPA Exam?

No, and this is a common misunderstanding among candidates. The CPA exam is only one of the "Three Es" requirements. You are required to fulfill the experience requirement to complete the process. Some of you may have gained prior experience that can be used toward fulfilling the experience requirements. In this case you can submit your license application shortly after the CPA exam.

Note

Make sure that it is possible for you to fulfill both the educational and experience requirement *before* filing the CPA exam application.

Is There a Time Limit between Passing the CPA Exam and Getting the CPA License?

There are cases where candidates choose to take the CPA exam before they are fully qualified for licensure. For example, the Montana state board allows candidates to take the CPA exam before they obtain a four-year bachelor's degree. On passing the CPA exam, the candidate should aim to complete the remaining studies to get the qualifying degree, the 150 credit hours, as well as the experience required to obtain the license.

Most state boards generally do not have a time limit on when you should complete all licensure requirements after the exam. There are exceptions to this rule. Check with your state board for details.

Note

If you take the CPA exam in one of the international testing centers, you must fulfill the working experience requirements within three years of passing the CPA exam no matter in which state you register. If this is a potential issue, refer to Chapter 3 for remedies.

What Are the Steps between Passing the Exam and Getting the License?

A number of states require candidates to pass a relatively simple CPA ethics exam after passing the Uniform CPA exam. A few states may require candidates to take an ethics course instead. More important, you need to fulfill the experience requirements before applying for the license.

I Do Not Plan to Practice Public Accounting. Can I Use the CPA Title to Enhance My Credentials without Getting the License?

In the United States, you cannot designate yourself as a CPA until you get the license. You can consider getting the CPA certificate (which is available in a few states only), which allows you to own a wall certificate and become an American Institute of Certified Public Accountants (AICPA) member, but there are restrictions on how you can use the CPA title on business cards and resumes.

How Exactly Can I Get Qualified?

Now that you have a general idea of the Uniform CPA Examination, let us see how you can get qualified to kick-start the process.

3

How to Get Qualified

This chapter focuses on the educational and experience requirements, the challenges faced by international candidates, and the ways to overcome the obstacles. This is an intense chapter—take the time to go through each step.

An Overview

In most countries, the professional accounting license is granted by a centralized governmental agency. In the United States, however, the CPA license is granted by the State Boards of Accountancy in 54 jurisdictions: the 50 states together with the District of Columbia, Guam, Puerto Rico, and the U.S. Virgin Islands.

The State Board of Accountancy is a regulatory body that oversees the accounting profession and establishes rules in assessing the eligibility of the CPA exam and CPA licensing candidates in its state.

Because each state board has the liberty to set its own regulations, the states have different rules on the educational and experience requirements for CPAs. In general, however, most states follow the "Three Es" requirements recommended by the American Institute of Certified Public Accountants (AICPA):

- Education: Graduate of a four-year bachelor's degree program with 150 credit hours of study, preferably with a concentration in accounting.
- Examination: Taking and passing the Uniform CPA Examination.

- Experience: One or more years of relevant experience supervised and/or verified by an active U.S. CPA licensee.

The Uniform CPA Examination

The CPA exam is officially known as the Uniform CPA Examination. Unlike the educational and experience requirements, the exam is centrally designed and graded by the AICPA, and is the same regardless of location.

The time required to fulfill these requirements and obtain the license can vary greatly depending on your education and professional background. It can take anywhere from a few months to several years to go through the following 13 steps:

1. Select a state that fits your educational background and work experience.
2. Send your transcripts to a foreign credential evaluation agency for evaluation (for graduates of non-U.S. universities only).
3. Fill in the application form from your chosen state.
4. Wait to receive the Notice to Schedule (NTS) from the National Association of State Boards of Accountancy (NASBA).
5. Schedule the exam at a Prometric center.
6. Research for a CPA review course and start studying.
7. Apply for U.S. visa if required, and arrange travel and accommodation.
8. Take the Uniform CPA Examination.
9. Wait for the result.
10. Depending on the state, you may need to take a CPA Ethics Exam after passing the Uniform CPA Examination.
11. Fulfill the experience requirements.
12. Apply for your wall certificate, CPA license, and AICPA membership.
13. Done!

The Educational Requirements

For domestic students majoring in accounting, the application process is straightforward because their academic program is designed

Prometric

Prometric is a company that specializes in administering computerized tests using their facilities (the Prometric centers) throughout the United States and in certain parts of the world. The Uniform CPA Examination is one of the many standardized tests administered by Prometric—expect to see lawyers, nurses, and all sorts of professionals taking the test with you.

to match the CPA exam's educational requirements of their corresponding state.

For international candidates, however, the same process can get complicated because their educational profiles do not usually match with the CPA exam requirements.

The Higher Education System in the United States

Before we begin, let us have a clear understanding of the education system in the United States and how this is related to your CPA exam application.

Four-Year Colleges and Universities   In the United States, a typical undergraduate program consists of four years of full-time education. The universities (more commonly known as colleges in the United States) use either the semester or quarter system to record the student's progress.

There are two semesters in each academic year. In each semester, students can take several courses with a varying number of semester hours (or credit hours). For example, if the course takes three hours a week, the student accumulates three credit hours. Students typically accumulate 30 credit hours in each academic year, and 120 credit hours on the graduation of a bachelor program.

The quarter system is also used in the United States. The quarter system means that the academic year is divided into four terms—fall, winter, spring, and summer—with the majority of students taking three terms per year. There are two terms (fall and spring) in the semester system. One semester hour is equivalent to 1.5 quarter hour.

Junior and Community Colleges   Besides the four-year bachelor program, there are junior or community colleges that offer two-year programs. These are known as *associate degrees* and are different from the full undergraduate program described earlier.

How the 150-Hour Rule Applies   In the context of the CPA exam qualifications, most states require 150 credit hours to ultimately get the license. One hundred and fifty credit hours translate into one full four-year bachelor's degree plus 30 additional credit hours. To meet this requirement, most accounting programs in the United States are either five-year programs (bachelor's degree plus one year of master's degree) or four-year accelerated programs so that the student can complete the required 150 credit hours within four years.

The educational level required for the U.S. CPA exam is one of the highest among the professional accounting examinations worldwide. It is therefore normal that your current educational level may not be enough for the typical 150-hour rule. Do not worry—you will likely find a solution to your situation below.

Breakdown of Educational Requirements

State boards look for the following to determine eligibility:

- Bachelor's degree and/or master's degree
- The 150-hour rule
- Number of credit hours in accounting and business courses

The Degree   All state boards require at least a bachelor's degree from a four-year undergraduate program.

If you graduate outside the United States, you can get your transcript evaluated by a foreign credential evaluation agency. These agencies look at your individual courses and "translate" each course into the U.S. equivalent so that the state boards can properly evaluate your educational level and assess the eligibility.

If you spent four years at your local university, you have a good chance to be deemed eligible in this regard.

If you come from a country where three-year degrees are prevalent, your degree will be considered an "associate degree," which is equivalent to a degree obtained from community colleges in the

United States. Since August 1, 2012, all state boards have stopped accepting candidates with associate degrees.

Unfortunately, candidates cannot make up a degree by taking one year's worth of classes in other educational institutions. Instead, the degree must be granted from an institution that offers four-year undergraduate programs.

Is there any solution to this? Yes—here are two options for you:

1. **Take a master's degree.** A two-year master's degree in a relevant subject will not only get you qualified for the "degree" requirement, but can also help you accumulate enough credit hours to fulfill the 150-hour rule.
2. **Transfer your credits**. You can explore ways to transfer your existing credits to a university offering a four-year accounting program and complete the four-year (and preferably five-year) program to fulfill the requirements.

Foreign Credential Evaluation Agencies

These agencies are companies independent of the state boards that provide services to convert non-U.S. degrees and credit hours to U.S. equivalents so that the state board can determine eligibility on the same basis. Some state boards approve one agency only while others may approve all agencies that are members of National Association of Credential Evaluation Services (NACES). You can see the list on the CPA exam application form.

The 150-Hour Rule   All but a few states have adopted the 150-hour rule: Candidates must accumulate 150 credit hours from accredited educational institutions in order to obtain a CPA license in the United States. Here are the exceptions to the rule:

- **California**: Currently grants licenses to those with 120 credit hours via "Pathway 1." Pathway 1 will be eliminated effective January 1, 2014, and all candidates must accumulate 150 credit hours for licensure.
- **Colorado**: A license is granted to those with 120 credit hours until July 1, 2015, after which all candidates must accumulate 150 credit hours.

- **Guam:** An "inactive license" is granted to those with 120 credit hours but candidates must have accounting concentration.
- **New Hampshire**: A license is granted to those with 120 credit hours until July 1, 2014, after which all candidates must accumulate 150 credit hours.

If you prefer not to take the additional credit hours, you can consider registering through one of these states. Note that each state has certain restrictions. We discuss these state requirements in detail later in this chapter.

Accounting and Business Courses   Candidates must meet the minimum number of accounting and business courses to become eligible for the exam.

A typical requirement is 24 credit hours of accounting courses and an additional 24 credit hours of general business courses. Some states ask for as many as 36 accounting credit hours while others ask for as few as 12 credit hours. Most states are fine with general accounting courses but some may require taking certain mandatory subjects, such as U.S. generally accepted auditing standards (GAAS) and U.S. federal taxation courses.

Note

U.S. specific courses such as U.S. federal taxation are likely not included in the local curriculum for international candidates. You have to choose between taking these courses separately and selecting another state.

In most cases the educational requirements for the exam and for the license is the same. There are a few exemptions; for example, Connecticut State Board asks for 24 accounting credit hours to sit for the exam but 36 credit hours to obtain the license. Double-check the details by visiting the NASBA and state board's websites, or call them directly.

A Note on Upper-Division Courses   Some states only count "upper-division" courses when they assess your eligibility. Upper-division means courses taken in the junior and senior years (i.e., third and fourth years) of

Note

If you prefer to complete the CPA exam before taking the master's degree and getting the full 150 credit hours, you are allowed to do that in a number of states.

These states allow candidates to sit for the exam as long as they have a four-year bachelor's degree and 120 credit hours. These candidates must submit the evidence of fulfilling the rest of the 150-hour educational requirements when they apply for the CPA license.

university. In other words, these states look for courses taken at the intermediate or advanced level.

The following examples demonstrate how this subtle rule can make or break your eligibility.

I have a reader, a BCom degree holder from India, who applied to sit for the exam in Montana. Based on the marksheet, she could easily get the 24 credit hours of accounting given that the coursework was heavily focused in accounting. However, only 14 credit hours were counted because the rest were deemed not to be upper-division classes.

Another reader, who has a three-year bachelor's degree and an MBA, was short a few accounting courses because the MBA program was finance-focused and most of the accounting classes were taught at introductory level.

Both of them were able to solve the issue by taking extra accounting courses online.

Note

I have a summary of CPA exam requirements by state at http://ipassthe cpaexam.com/cpa-exam-requirements/. This page is regularly updated but you are advised to get the latest information by clicking the source links that are located at the bottom of each post.

You can contact the state board regarding eligibility for the CPA exam and licensure. For states that have outsourced the CPA exam application administration to NASBA, your queries may be forwarded to the NASBA state representatives.

An Interview with Rob

Rob is an accounting professional living and working in California. He is originally from the Philippines.

1. **Why are you interested in getting the CPA qualification?**

   I know that the CPA title will open doors for me here in the United States. I am a CPA in the Philippines and I had opportunities that could never have occurred without my title.

2. **What is your educational background?**

   I have a bachelor's degree in accountancy in the Philippines.

3. **Which state did you apply to, and why?**

   California. This where I reside and plan to practice my profession.

4. **Which foreign credential evaluation agency did you go through?**

   Academic Credentials Evaluation Institute (ACEI). I remember choosing them because they have reasonable fees. I sent them a notarized copy of my transcript and paid about US$200 for my evaluation plus an extra copy.

5. **How many educational credits did you get from the evaluation?**

   One hundred and eighty-seven units. I took a lot of subjects back then!

6. **What do you think of the evaluation agency?**

   It took about two to three weeks before I received my evaluation. I can say they have good service. I was not in a hurry, but I appreciate that they have a site online where you can check the status of your application. I am pretty satisfied with their service (they sent the "sealed" copy to the California Board of Accountancy) and I got approved to sit for the CPA exam.

7. **When did you apply?**
   - Transcripts sent to ACEI—June 17.
   - Application to the CA Board of Accountancy (paid the US$100 application fee)—June 21.
   - Got the approval to sit from CA Board of Accountancy—August 6.

8. **When did you get your NTS?**

   November 24. It took a long time only because I kept delaying my payment of the examination fee to NASBA so that I had more time to study.

9. **Any additional information that you would like to share?**

Plan ahead of time. Do not pay for the sections you are not ready to take. NTS (Notice to Schedule) is only good for 6 to 12 months, depending on the state where you apply. Consider paying only the reapplication fee (about US$50) to take the rest of the sections, in consideration of the expiration of the sections that you passed, of course. Start planning . . . *now*. Good luck!

Note   California is a popular state for candidates with international backgrounds, but this state is not for you if you do not have a social security number (SSN). Specifically, the California state board allows non-SSN holders to sit for the exam, but only SSN holders will be granted the CPA license. We discuss the topic of a social security number later in this chapter.

The Experience Requirements

Getting and verifying the relevant work experience is a critical step toward the CPA licensure. Most candidates, however, do not pay attention to this requirement until after passing the CPA exam.

If you live in the United States and plan to work in public accounting, this requirement should not be of particular concern, because your experience will most likely qualify you.

However, if you live outside the United States and especially in countries where there are few active U.S. CPA license holders, or if you do not plan to work in public accounting in the foreseeable future, you should pay extra attention during (and not after) the state board selection process because it has big implications on whether you can ultimately obtain the license in your chosen state.

What Is Counted as Relevant Experience, and What Is Not

Although there are variations from state to state on what is required for work experience, these general rules apply:

- The experience should be relevant.
- The experience must be verified and/or supervised by a U.S. CPA or equivalent.
- The license of this CPA should be active during the time of the supervision.

Relevance   State boards have different rules when it comes to the relevancy of work experience. A few state boards only recognize experience gained in public accounting and specify the minimum number of billable hours obtained for audit work. Most states accept general accounting experience, such as working in the financial or management accounting department of a company, internal audit, governmental accounting, or as accounting teaching professionals in academia.

Apart from the job nature, the number of years in the industry can also be quite different. Most state boards ask for one year of experience, while some require up to five years of experience in cases where they determine your experience is not as relevant.

If you are not an auditor and have no interest in getting into public accounting, or if you believe it is difficult to land a job at a CPA firm at this stage of your career, then you should select a state that allows a more general definition of relevant experience.

Note

To find out what it takes to get a job in public accounting versus nonpublic accounting, you can check out my post on this subject at http://ipassthecpaexam.com/public-accounting-vs-private/.

CPA Equivalent   A valid verifier of your work experience should be a CPA. This CPA should be U.S.-qualified and a CPA license holder instead of a CPA certificate holder (we talk about the difference below). The license should also be valid during the period when you accumulate your experience.

Some states allow "CPA equivalent" but the definition varies from state to state. If your supervisor is a Chartered Accountant (CA) from Canada or Australia, this person will most likely be considered a valid CPA equivalent. Some states recognize accountants who are CA/CPAs of countries with reciprocal agreements with the United States, although a few do not specify the rules and may be determined on a case-by-case basis.

CA/CPAs from other countries will likely not be able to verify your experience. International candidates should pay special attention to this rule.

Verification versus Supervision   Many of you may have worked outside the United States and have not been supervised by U.S. CPAs. In this case you may consider states that allow verification instead of strictly supervision of experience.

A number of states, such as Montana, Indiana, and Washington, allow candidates to get their experience verified by a U.S. CPA whom they know. A few other states, such as North Dakota and Virginia, require the supervisor to verify the experience but this supervisor does not need to be a CPA. These rules add a lot of flexibility in the verification process.

> **Note**
>
> It is commonly believed that the experience has to be accumulated within a U.S. territory. This has not been the case. It will work as long as the experience can be verified and/or supervised by a person trusted by the state board (i.e., a U.S. CPA or equivalent).

An Interview with Annu

Annu had years of financial accounting experience before moving to the United States with her husband. They are originally from India but are now living in Washington. As an H4 visa holder, Annu does not have a social security number and is barred from working in the United States.

1. **Why are you interested in getting the CPA?**
   I would like to enhance my accounting knowledge with a widely and globally accepted professional degree within the shortest span of time.
2. **What is your educational background?**
   I have a BA degree in accounting and MBA in finance.
3. **Which state did you apply to, and why?**
   Washington. I am residing here and my husband is working here. I believe it would be easy for me to practice here.
4. **Which foreign credential evaluation agency did you go through, and why?**
   ECE. They have a rush service that does not require original credentials to perform their evaluation. I got my evaluation report and original certificates within one week.

5. **How many credits did you get from the evaluation?**
    One hundred and sixty hours, including the MBA program.
6. **What do you think of the process?**
    It has been smooth for me. I applied for a 15-day rush service but I got my credential evaluation within one week. The evaluation cost is also reasonable.
7. **When did you get your NTS?**
    I got the NTS in the same month, within one to two weeks.

Note   If you are well-qualified for the CPA exam, you have a chance to get approved quickly, as in Annu's case here. Most states ask candidates to allow four weeks for processing. Some popular states may ask you to wait as long as eight weeks.

Annu is not allowed to work as an H4 visa holder, but her work experience in India can be verified by a U.S. CPA who knows her personally. Under the rules in the state of Washington, this verifier does not need to be her supervisor as long as the verifier has been an active CPA licensee for five years.

Citizenship and Residency Requirements

There are additional requirements for citizenship, residency, and the availability of a social security number.

Citizenship and State Residency

These states/jurisdictions only accept candidates who are U.S. citizens:

- Alabama
- North Carolina
- Puerto Rico

These states only accept applications from their own residents or employees, including resident noncitizens such as international students and H1B visa holders:

- Idaho
- Kansas
- Louisiana
- Minnesota

- Missouri
- Nebraska
- Oklahoma
- Rhode Island
- Wyoming

The rest of the states welcome citizens and residents from other countries.

Social Security Number

A social security number (SSN) is a 9-digit number issued to U.S. citizens, permanent residents, and temporary workers in order to track these individuals for social security purposes.

The Certified Public Accountant (CPA) profession is regulated and most state boards make use of SSNs to monitor their licensees.

If you have not been living or working in the United States, you will not have been issued an SSN and this will bar you from getting the CPA license in certain states such as California and Florida. Note, however, that some states waive this requirement if the international candidate submits a signed affidavit or a letter to the state board explaining the situation.

The issue of SSNs can possibly be solved with a simple letter and thus should not be your first consideration when selecting a state for the CPA exam application. You can make the preliminary screening based on the educational and experience requirements (which most often is the bottleneck), then double-check the rules on SSNs before making the final decision.

Taking Advantage of the Differences

Although sifting through the different CPA exam requirements by state is a frustrating process, you may be encouraged to know that tens of thousands of international candidates of various backgrounds managed to get qualified and pass the CPA exam, all because of these differences.

One of the primary purposes of this book is to guide you through the maze and tell you exactly what you need to do to get qualified. To get started, let me clarify some of the technical terms that you may have seen during your own research.

CPA Certificate versus CPA License

These terms are confusing because they are defined differently across jurisdictions. Generally, the "CPA certificate" is a recognition given to candidates after passing the CPA exam. This allows them to join the AICPA but only use the CPA title in a restrictive manner.

A "CPA license" is a full recognition that allows the license holder to sign audit reports, set up his own CPA firm, and verify experience of other candidates for the purpose of CPA licensing. This CPA license is also known as the *permit* in a few states.

Note that most states have stopped issuing CPA certificates and thus the difference between certificate and license has become irrelevant. In these states, there is no longer any formal recognition granted to candidates on the passing of the CPA exam. A candidate should aim to complete the whole process by gaining the experience and getting the full license.

There are, however, a few remaining jurisdictions that give out CPA certificates. They are known as the *two-tier states*.

Two-Tier States

These few states grant the CPA designation in two tiers—candidates are qualified for the first tier by demonstrating sound accounting knowledge, typically by fulfilling the educational requirements and passing the CPA exam. These candidates receive a CPA certificate.

The second tier is a full CPA license, which the candidate can obtain after gaining the required experience.

Note

As of first quarter of 2013, Alabama, Connecticut, Hawaii, Kansas, Montana, Nebraska, and Oklahoma are the remaining two-tier states. In practice, Guam can also be considered a de facto two-tier state due to the availability of an "inactive" CPA license.

Although I could not find the relevant information, the District of Columbia is also marked as a two-tier jurisdiction. Refer to NASBA's website for more information: www.nasba.org/licensure/substantialequivalency/.

The two-tier system was prevalent in the past: The CPA certificate was originally designed for accountants who wanted the title for credentials only without the intention to practice public accounting. However, because the general public could not differentiate the subtle difference between CPA license and certificate, many states have stopped issuing CPA certificate and become "one-tier" states.

An Interview with Susan

Susan is a CPA candidate from Singapore who obtained her education in Australia and work experience in China.

1. **Why are you interested in getting the CPA qualification?**

    I wanted to enhance my eight years of accounting working experience in a multinational corporation and I was deciding between a master's degree and the CPA qualification.

    While working in China, a friend introduced me to the CPA designation and after some researching, I realized the flexibility of this qualification in that the education requirements are different among the various states, and that there are four windows in a year to sit for the exam with test centers now in Guam, Japan, and the Middle East to cater to international candidates like myself. To top it off, I was able to obtain a prestigious professional qualification in the shortest time.

2. **What is your educational background?**

    I have a three-year bachelor's degree in banking and finance from an Australian university. To fulfill the educational requirement, I took extra accounting and audit courses online through the University of North Alabama (UNA).

3. **Which state did you apply to, and why?**

    Montana is my choice because it allows me to take the exam with an associate degree (although I understand I need to fulfill the 150 credit hours later on). It also gives out certificates without the public accounting working experience requirement.

4. **Which foreign credential evaluation agency did you go through?**

    I went through Foreign Academic Credentials Service (FACS) as it was the only agency recognized by Montana.

5. **How many educational credits did you get from the evaluation?**

    I got 96 credit hours that can be considered an associate degree. I got 21 semester hours of accounting courses but not all are considered upper-division courses. I took extra courses to make up nine extra credit hours to fulfill the minimum requirements.

6. **What do you think of the evaluation agency?**

It took about 12 weeks for FACS to get back to me. Although I read on the Internet that response tends to be slower during the summer months, I was still quite nervous about not getting the results in time. Nevertheless I was glad that the results turned out to be what I expected. Response time by FACS was indeed prompt.

7. **How long did it take you from application to getting the NTS?**

Five months.

Note A number of states recognize FACS as the only foreign credential evaluation service provider. Although FACS is one of the most affordable, it takes the longest processing time without the option of a rush service.

For those who must go through FACS, expect six to eight weeks (up to 12 weeks as in Susan's case) of turnaround time. You should also make every effort to fulfill all the educational requirements before applying to the evaluation agency because a reevaluation costs money and further delays the process.

IQEX—International Qualification Examination

The IQEX exam is designed for candidates who are members of non-U.S. professional associations that have entered into mutual recognition agreements (MRA) with the International Qualifications Appraisal Board (IQAB).

MRA have been established with the statutory accounting bodies in:

- Australia (Chartered Accountants only)
- Canada (Chartered Accountants only)
- Hong Kong
- Ireland
- Mexico
- New Zealand

These candidates are required to submit a letter from the accountancy body to get qualified for IQEX. The candidate benefits not only from the simpler application process, but also a much shorter version of the exam—only the Regulation (REG) section of the exam will be tested. This exam is offered in the United States and Canada.

Note that only candidates who are educated in the country where they become a CA can qualify for IQEX. For example, an accountant completed his study in Malaysia and obtained his Chartered Accountancy in Canada. In this case he is not eligible for taking the IQEX but he can go through the Uniform CPA exam. Refer to my post on IQEX for more information and links to the source documents: http://ipassthecpaexam.com/iqex/.

An Interview with Ryan

Ryan is originally from China but he received his bachelor's degree in Hong Kong. He has been working in one of the Big 4 since graduation and has become a member of HKICPA, the statutory accounting body in Hong Kong. The HKICPA signed an MRA with the IQAB in November 2012.

1. **Why are you interested in getting the CPA qualification?**

   I am working in one of the Big 4 accounting firms in Hong Kong. While it is not necessary to get a U.S. CPA for promotion within the Hong Kong office, I would like to get the qualification as proof of my commitment to public accounting, and to pave the way to work in the U.S. if I can arrange an internal transfer.

   I travel a lot for business and have very limited time to study. I am glad to be able to go through IQEX because the IQEX exam is a much shorter version of the CPA exam.

2. **What is your educational background?**

   I was born and raised in China but graduated from a university in Hong Kong.

3. **Which state did you apply to, and why?**

   Illinois, because I have friends in Canada who applied for IQEX through this state. Also, Illinois recognizes working experience I gained in Hong Kong because my supervisor, who is a member of the HKICPA, can be a qualifying verifier.

4. **Which foreign credential evaluation agency did you go through?**

   There is no need to go through the credential evaluation agency. I only need to get a letter of support from HKICPA, of which I am a member.

5. Any additional information that you would like to share?
You can go to Canada to take the IQEX exam. From my colleagues' experience, the Canadian tourist visa is either not required or easier to get when compared to the visa to the United States. This is one less hassle to worry about for this exam.

Note When Ryan graduated, Hong Kong was using the three-year university system and therefore he would not be able to get qualified without going through IQEX. Hong Kong has since switched to a four-year bachelor degree system and therefore the current university graduates can take the CPA exam without becoming a HKICPA member.

Now, let us look at some common challenges faced by international candidates and possible remedies to overcome the obstacles.

Non-U.S. Accounting Degree: Four Years

A typical bachelor's of accountancy or bachelor's of business administration in accounting degree falls into this category. The good news is that you have fulfilled one of the most essential prerequisites—the minimum degree requirement.

Unless you went through an accelerated accounting program (which are available in certain countries such as the Philippines), you are likely lacking a number of credit hours to fulfill the 150-hour rule.

You have two choices.

Make Up for the Remaining Credit Hour by Taking Additional Courses Most states allow you to take courses in any accredited educational institutions including community colleges and online courses. It is prudent however to double-check with your chosen state for any restrictions. We go over the tips on selecting these courses in the section for nonaccounting majors.

Select a State That Only Requires 120 Credit Hours to Get Qualified We discussed the few states/jurisdictions that do not follow the 150-hour rule, at least for a few more years. These states/jurisdictions are:

- California
- Colorado
- Guam
- New Hampshire

My Recommendations   Guam is my favorite choice if:

- You are an accounting major but are not able to get your experience verified.
- You do not have a social security number.
- You do not mind getting an inactive license. This inactive license prevents you from designating yourself as a CPA within Guam territories.

California works if:

- You have a social security number.
- You can pass the CPA exam before the change of rule in January 1, 2014.
- You plan to work for at least two years in accounting.
- You have nonpublic accounting work experience. It is accepted in California but it has to be supervised and verified by an active U.S. CPA licensee. If it is public accounting work experience, it can possibly be verified by a CPA equivalent.

New Hampshire is a good choice if:

- You have few accounting courses (only 12 credit hours are required).
- You can pass the CPA exam before the change of rule in July 1, 2014.
- You plan to work in accounting for at least two years.
- You have public or nonpublic accounting experience. Either one is accepted in New Hampshire but it has to be supervised and verified by an active U.S. CPA licensee, or equivalent.

Go for Colorado if:

- The above states do not work for one reason or another.
- You can take three credit hours of an auditing course covering U.S. GAAS before applying for the exam.

Non-U.S. Accounting Degree: Two to Three Years

The three-year degree is prevalent in the United Kingdom and commonwealth countries such as Australia, Hong Kong (pre-334 scheme), and India. The popular bachelor of commerce (B.com) degree falls into this category.

Three-Year Degree Only   Unfortunately a three-year degree is not sufficient to pass the eligibility test. I recommend that you explore a two-year master's degree program to get you qualified both on the degree qualification and the 150-hour rule.

Three-Year Degree Plus Professional Accounting Qualifications   A few years ago, Chartered Accountants were automatically qualified to take the exam in a few states such as Colorado and Michigan. As far as I know, all state boards now consider chartered accountancy a professional qualification instead of an educational qualification, thus are no longer granting the exemption. Specifically, the Indian Chartered Accountancy and ACCA are no longer seen as equivalent to a four-year bachelor's degree, and their coursework can no longer be considered toward the 150-hour rule.

You are in the same situation as having a three-year degree. Consider taking a two-year master's degree in a relevant field to make it work.

The same applies to other professional certification such as CFA, CMA, and CIA. The only exception applies to accountants eligible to take IQEX.

Three-Year Degree Plus One Year of a Master's Degree   In theory this is equivalent to a four-year bachelor's degree with 120 credit hours. If your master's degree is two years and you are halfway through, you may take the exam now but I strongly recommend that you wait until the completion of the program to apply for the licensure, because this will make you fully eligible by fulfilling the 150-hour rule.

Three-Year Degree Plus Two Years of a Master's Degree   This will likely work as long as you have enough qualified accounting courses. Note that if the master's degree is taken as a correspondence (i.e., long-distance) course from an educational institution that is not regionally accredited, the degree may not be counted.

The vast majority of universities outside the United States are not regionally accredited. Keep this in mind if you are contemplating a master's degree with the intention to get a U.S. CPA license in the future.

Courses taken in a classroom setting from nonregionally accredited educational institutions are generally fine.

Nonaccounting Majors

It used to be relatively easy for nonaccounting majors to get qualified for the CPA exam, but state boards are now asking for a minimum number of accounting and business courses, which has substantially increased the barrier of entry.

The good news is that you can make up for these classes without getting an additional accounting degree—an investment that is costly and time-consuming, but doable if you are determined to get the CPA title.

Accounting classes offered in community colleges and online courses are generally more affordable or more flexible. Although most state boards accept these courses, you should double-check the fine print. For example, New York and Alabama State Boards may not recognize "core accounting courses" such as financial accounting or auditing taken in community colleges.

There are a number of states that ask for fewer accounting courses:

- New Hampshire: 12 credit hours
- Alaska: 15 credit hours
- Maine: 15 credit hours
- Hawaii: 18 credit hours
- Georgia: 20 credit hours
- Massachusetts: 21 credit hours

Note that these states may have stricter rules on work experience to compensate for the relatively lenient educational requirements in accounting. For example, Maine requires two years of public accounting experience, which could be tough to fulfill if the candidate is a nonaccounting major.

Note

On my website, I list out the pros and cons of community colleges and provide suggestions on how to make up for the credit hours. Go here for details: http://ipassthecpaexam.com/extra-credits-for-cpa-exam-requirements/.

Nondegree Candidates with More Than 15 Years of Relevant Experience

There are seasoned accounting professionals who possess many years of practical experience but never obtained a bachelor's degree. They may consider registering through New York.

New York State Board allows candidates to sit for the exam if they have 15 or more years of experience in public accounting. The work should involve the application of U.S. generally accepted accounting principles (GAAP) and generally accepted auditing standards (GAAS), and contain substantial exposure to auditing and financial statement preparation. The experience must be earned under direct supervision by a U.S. CPA or a New York State Public Accountant.

Candidates Who Do Not Work under a U.S. CPA or Get Relevant Experience

Many international candidates work in a country where there are few actively licensed U.S. CPAs. In this case it makes it difficult to fulfill the experience requirement where candidates are required to work under the supervision of one. This also applies to H4 visa holders who are not authorized to work in the United States.

I have some options for you.

Go for the CPA Certificate   If you are getting the CPA title for credentials only, you can consider getting the CPA certificate. Read carefully the restrictions and prepare to respect the rules.

Select a State That Requires Only Verification versus Supervision   This flexibility can help you locate a valid verifier more easily. Note that the verifier, while not necessarily your direct supervisor, should know you personally and be in the position to comment on the nature of your work in detail.

You can also select a state that allows your supervisor and verifier of your experience to be a non-CPA.

Select a State/Jurisdiction That Does Not Require Work Experience

- **Colorado**: Candidates with 150 credit hours or more can opt for "education in lieu of experience" route to get the CPA license without work experience. Note that this rule will become obsolete in 2015.

- **Guam**: You can apply for the "inactive license," which does not require work experience. The restriction is that you cannot designate yourself as a CPA within Guam's territory.
- **Massachusetts**: You can apply for the "nonreporting license"—for candidates with graduate degrees, no experience is required. A nonreporting license allows you to perform all accounting services except issuing reports on financial statements.

Candidates without a Social Security Number

By default, candidates are required to fill in the social security number in the application form because this is one of the best tools for a state board to regulate its licensee.

Here are the states that firmly adhere to this rule:

- States that require citizenship.
- States that require residency—in theory, all residents should have social security numbers. If you are one of the rare exceptions (e.g., H4 visa holders), you can seek advice from the state board.
- California, Nevada, Tennessee—the rule says that non-SSN holders are allowed to sit for the exam but not allowed to obtain a license.
- Florida, Virginia, West Virginia—not allowed to sit for the exam and apply for the license without an SSN.

The rules are not as clear-cut in other states. Some may allow exemptions as long as you have a valid reason, such as the fact that you live outside the United States and have never been issued a social security number. In this case you will be asked to fill in an affidavit or write a letter to explain the situation to the board.

I encourage you to shortlist the states by the education and work experience requirements before checking the rule on social security number.

Taking the Exam at International Sites: The Pros and Cons

International CPA candidates, including U.S. citizens who reside in foreign countries, have longed for an opportunity to take the CPA exam closer to home. Although we get all excited about the current and future international CPA exam sites, there are implications if you choose to take the exam outside the United States.

The Similarities

The good news is that the education and work experience requirements, as well as the format, content, and schedule of the CPA exam are the same as those offered within the U.S. jurisdictions. Even the test-taking experience is similar because the exam sites are run by Prometric.

The Differences

Candidates have slightly fewer choices of states because not all states participate in this international administration of the CPA exam, notably California and Delaware.

For candidates taking the exam at these international sites, they must fulfill the experience requirements and obtain the license within three years or lose the exam credit, while there is no such rule if you take the exam within U.S. jurisdictions. This may be a challenge if your country does not have many active U.S. CPA licensees.

There are two remedies for your consideration.

You can aim for CPA certificate-only by registering through one of the two-tier states. Be prepared for the fact that after the three years are over, you will not be able to "upgrade" to a full license even if you have a chance to work under a U.S. CPA.

You can also consider selecting a state where the state board requires a verification of experience versus strict supervision. This flexibility will greatly increase your chance to get the experience verified and become a CPA within three years.

CPA Exam Qualification Quiz

Here is a short quiz to test your ability to navigate the various state board rules.

Questions

1. Olivia graduated with a three-year bachelor's degree from the United Kingdom. She wants to take the CPA exam and is willing to make up the remaining year (i.e., 30 credit hours)

by taking nondegree courses from a U.S. university. Can she get qualified?

2. Liang majored in accounting from a four-year university in China. He is working in the investment team of a hedge fund but wants to get a CPA title for credential only. He has no social security number, does not plan to get accounting working experience, and does not want to take extra courses to get 150 credit hours. Can he get a CPA qualification?

3. Muhammad works in Egypt and he does not want to travel to the United States for the CPA exam. Is it possible for him to take the exam at a non-U.S. location, and if so, which one?

4. Julie is an Indian chartered accountant and has recently become a member of CICA in Canada using the Reciprocal Membership Agreement between ICAI and CICA. Julie obtained her education in India. As a member of CICA, can she take the IQEX instead of the Uniform CPA exam?

5. Max has a master's degree in statistics and took some accounting courses during college. He has 15 credit hours of accounting courses, which is sufficient to fulfill the minimum requirement in Maine. To get the license in Maine, he needs to work for two years in public accounting after passing the exam. He does not want to work in public accounting, so he plans to transfer the exam credit to another state (e.g., Illinois) where the work experience requirement is more flexible. Is it possible?

Answers

1. No. The nondegree courses are counted toward the educational requirement as extra credit hours, but Julie still needs a four-year bachelor's degree or equivalent to get qualified. If she takes the same courses under a degree program (e.g., a master's degree), or if she transfers her U.K. credits to a four-year university and then graduates from this university, then it will work.

2. Yes. Liang can register through Guam and choose to obtain the inactive license. On passing the CPA exam, he cannot designate himself as a CPA within Guam territory but he can get his wall certificate and is eligible to become an AICPA member.

3. Yes. As a long-term resident of Egypt, Muhammad can take the exam in the Prometric centers in any of these four countries: Bahrain, Kuwait, Lebanon, and the United Arab Emirates.

4. No, Julie must take the Uniform CPA exam instead of the IQEX. Even though CICA has signed a reciprocal agreement with the IQAB in the United States, only candidates who are educated in the reciprocal country where she becomes a CA can qualify for IQEX. Julie obtained her education in India instead of Canada and therefore is not qualified for the IQEX.

5. The rule of thumb regarding exam credit transfer is that the candidate should have fulfilled the eligibility requirements of the transferee (Illinois) before the CPA exam. In other words, you are not allowed to "game the system." Because the Illinois state board requires more than 15 credit hours of accounting courses, Max is unlikely to be able to transfer the exam credit from Maine to Illinois. There may be exceptions to this general rule but candidates should check with the state boards before applying.

Note

If you find the rules confusing, do not worry—help is only a click away! If you have any questions or need guidance on a unique situation, you are most welcome to drop me a note on my CPA exam discussion forum at http://forum.ipassthecpaexam.com/.

Final Thoughts

For most international candidates, the application process is likely the most time-consuming and frustrating part of the CPA journey. In comparison, the actual studying for the exam seems easier!

In the next chapter we go over the steps after getting approved for the exam.

4

Getting Ready

Once you have selected a state where you can get qualified, you are in much better control. In this chapter I walk you through the following steps:

- Budgeting
- Submitting the application
- Scheduling the exam
- Arranging travel and accommodation
- Visualizing the experience at the testing center
- Waiting for the result

Budgeting

The CPA exam is a substantial investment of time, effort, and money. Before making the decision to pursue the CPA, let us look at how much it can cost for the entire process.

The Examination Fee

This is the fee for first-time applicants in 2013:

- FAR: $190.35
- AUD: $190.35
- BEC: $171.25
- REG: $171.25
- Total: $723.20

Additional fees include:

- Application fee: Applicable to all first-timers and some retakers depending on the state, ranging from $30 to $200.
- Registration fee: Ranges from $50 to $150 depending on the number of exam sections you take. You can save up by registering multiple sections in one go.
- If you fail the exam and require a retake, you will have to pay the registration fee and examination fee again.

Total fees: $900–$1,100

CPA Review Courses

Although not mandatory, CPA review courses greatly increase your chance of passing success. The cost ranges anywhere from $260 for a set of CPA review books to full-blown guided review courses at more than $3,000. You should select a course based on your background, budget, and learning style.

CPA Ethics Exam

Around 35 states and jurisdictions require candidates to take a CPA ethics exam after passing the Uniform CPA exam. If you take the one administered by the American Institute of Certified Public Accountants (AICPA) (chosen by most states), it costs around $150.

Recurring Fees

- **Licensing fee**: It depends on the state, but the range is roughly $50 to $300. The fee is paid on an annual or biannual basis.
- **Continuing education**: All active CPA licensees are required to take a certain number of continuing professional education (CPE) courses. Note that this is a recurring cost.

Total Expense You Should Expect

Let us take the midpoint of the above expenses:

- Examination fee: $1,000
- Review course: $1,800
- CPA ethics exam: $150

- Licensing fee: $150
- Total: $3,100

Additional Expenses for International Candidates

- Foreign credential evaluation: $100–$300.
- Additional courses to fulfill the 150-hour rule, if required: $400 per course (three credit hours) at the minimum.
- Additional examination fee if you sit for the exam at the international test centers: approximately $120–$160 per section.
- Travel and accommodation: this can vary greatly.
- Visa application.

Is the CPA Title Worth This Much?

The expense is around $3,000 for domestic candidates and could be considerably more for international candidates.

Although getting the CPA is expensive, this investment can produce an impressive return if the designation can help you get a more stable income, a more interesting job, more frequent promotions, and a faster track toward financial freedom.

Submitting the Application

The application form is quite detailed but as long as you have the documents ready, you should be able to complete the process within half an hour.

Step 1: Fill in the Application Form

The following states and territories outsource the application administration work to the National Association of State Boards of Accountancy (NASBA) (you can fill in the application online at cpacentral.nasba.org): Alaska, Colorado, Connecticut, Delaware, Florida, Georgia, Hawaii, Indiana, Iowa, Kansas, Louisiana, Maine, Massachusetts, Michigan, Minnesota, Missouri, Montana, Nebraska, New Hampshire, New Jersey, New Mexico, New York, Ohio, Pennsylvania, Puerto Rico, Rhode Island, South Carolina, Tennessee, Utah, Vermont, Washington, and Wisconsin.

The state boards of the following jurisdictions administer the application process. You can find a link to their application form in their respective websites: Alabama, Arizona, Arkansas, California, District of Columbia, Guam, Idaho, Illinois, Kentucky, Maryland, Mississippi, Nevada, North Carolina, North Dakota, Oklahoma, Oregon, South Dakota, Texas, U.S. Virgin Islands, Virginia, West Virginia, and Wyoming.

Similarly, your name on the application form should appear exactly the same as the one on the identification you will be bring on the exam day.

A reader had a devastating story to tell. She got married recently, enjoyed her job at a reputable regional CPA firm, and had fully prepared for her first section of the CPA exam. On the exam day when she handed in her ID for inspection, she realized that the name on her driver's license (still with her maiden name) was different from that on the Notice to Schedule (NTS). She begged and begged but the proctor did not let her in. She had to repay the examination fees, restudy the materials, and take the exam in the next testing window.

I also have my own experience to share. On my passport, I have my Chinese name as my first name and English name (Stephanie) as the middle name, but during college I had it reversed out of convenience. In the CPA exam application, I used the name on my passport and asked my school to send the transcript to the state board directly. Because the name was slightly different and they were sent separately, the state board was unable to locate my transcript. It took many stressful phone calls to get things fixed.

The only exception to this exact-match rule is the middle initial being substituted for the middle name (e.g., the NTS reads John A. Doe, but the name on the candidate's license reads John Albert Doe), or vice versa.

Step 2: Pay the Fees

The easiest way is to register and pay online via credit card (VISA, MasterCard, or Discover). Some state boards collect both the application fee and examination fee at the time of application, while others may only ask for the application fee and you need to pay the examination fee to NASBA directly. In either case there is clear instruction on the application form.

Pay only for exam sections that you are ready to take within your NTS validation period. In most states, the NTS is valid for six months, counting from the day it is issued. The following states have a different validation period:

- Ninety days from application date: Texas
- Nine months from NTS issue date: California, Hawaii, Louisiana, Utah
- Twelve months from NTS issue date: North Dakota, South Dakota, Virginia

Step 3: Wait to Receive the NTS

Once you have completed and sent the application form, you will be informed of the processing time. Most states process the application within four weeks but big states such as California and Illinois can take a few weeks longer.

The state board will also ask how you would like to receive your NTS. Email is the most convenient in my opinion, but you can choose to have the NTS faxed or mailed to you.

The NTS prints your name as well as the examination section identification number for each approved section of the exam. This number is also used as the "launch code" (i.e., password) to log in on the exam day.

Scheduling the Exam

Once you receive the NTS, you can schedule your examination. Here are the options.

Online Appointment

I recommend that you schedule the exam online at the Prometric website, because this is the fastest and most flexible way to make, reschedule, or cancel appointments. Have the NTS ready for you to type in the examination section identification number.

Note

The Prometric system does not alert you about overlapping appointment times. Pay special attention if you are to schedule multiple sections in a day. Allow at least 30 minutes for the check-in time between sections.

Appointment by Phone

Alternatively, you can call 800-580-9648 (Candidate Services Call Center) and speak to a customer service officer to schedule the exam.

Taking the Exam at International Locations

There is an "Apply to Test Internationally" link at the NASBA website (under CPA exam international) that prompts you to pay the additional fees. Have your NTS as well as your valid passport or national ID card ready, as you need to type in the information to register.

After the completion of the registration process, you need to wait at least 24 hours before you can continue the standard process and schedule your exam at the Prometric website.

Note

It is best to schedule the exam in the morning when you are fresh with a good night's sleep. While an exam in the afternoon may allow for some last-minute studying, it will drain your energy and the anxiety will make it difficult to concentrate.

When Should I Schedule the Exam?

The CPA exam administrators recommend that you schedule at least 45 days before the desired test dates in order to receive first choice of date, time, and location.

In reality, you may worry about the possibility of not getting ready by that date. You can wait until a month before your desired test date, but this will inevitably increase the chance of the slot being taken by other candidates. The latest date to schedule your appointment is five days before the desired test date.

I recommend that you schedule a time first and reschedule if you need more time to study.

Is It Possible to Reschedule?

Yes, but with the following conditions:

- Thirty days or more in advance: no penalty
- Six to 29 days in advance: penalty of $35

- One to 5 days in advance: penalty of $66–$150 depending on the exam section and whether it is a domestic or international exam site
- Less than 24 hours: impossible to reschedule and you will have to reapply

If you encounter visa rejection, hardship, an acute medical condition, or other extreme circumstance, you may contact your state board for a possible extension.

Travel and Accommodation

Unless you live in a big city, chances are that you do not live or work close to a Prometric center. In this case you need special arrangements for transportation or even a few nights' stay at a hotel. For international candidates, more advanced planning is required to secure air tickets, local transportation, hotels, and possibly visa applications. You may also want to arrive a few days early to adjust to the jet lag and the weather.

I have a list of "items to bring" in Appendix B, but you should pack according to your own personal need. For example, bring:

- Special medication, if needed.
- Coffee/tea that you must have for every morning.
- Comfort food/favorite snack to keep you happy before and after the exam.
- Your own soap and shampoo—this is especially important if you stay at a budget hotel.

Where to Stay   This largely depends on your budget, the location of the hotel, and whether you have friends or family near a testing center. Allow enough time to research and choose the accommodation that fits your budget and style.

When I took the exam in Guam, I chose to stay at a five-star hotel (the most affordable one) because I did not want to worry about the quality of the room, food, and service. Other candidates may pick the budget hotels that are more affordable, with lots of local restaurants around and closer to the test center.

If you are traveling from abroad and have friends or family in the United States, you may want to plan for a visit after taking the exam. You may even explore whether you can stay at their place and pick a Prometric center nearby to save accommodation cost. Remember, you can register in one state and physically take the exam in another.

> **Note**
>
> If you can afford it, consider staying an additional night at the hotel (i.e., the night on the exam day) so you do not need to worry about when to check out the hotel room and how to store your luggage after checkout. Also, you can enjoy the swimming pool and a nice bath after the exam.

What to Wear   Since the main (and possibly only) purpose of your trip is to take the exam, you should wear the most comfortable clothes and shoes, and leave the high heels, jewelry, and fancy clothes at home. You may also want to wear clothes with a simple design—avoid clothes with lots of frills and pockets as it may take you more time at the security check at the testing center.

What to Eat   If you are traveling to a new place, it is tempting to try some new food. This is an excellent idea except that you should do that *after* the exam.

My hotel had the most delicious tuna sashimi that I have ever tasted, and it was available at the breakfast buffet every day. I could not help eating lots of it but in retrospect, I ran a big risk of stomach upset on the exam day. I was lucky to be fine but this is something you should keep in mind.

For international candidates, I recommend that you bring some local food, such as kim chi instant noodles (but the food has to be in dehydrated form). I know you will thank me for this!

What to Do One Day before the Exam Day   Here is a suggestion on how you can make this a productive day:

Note

If you live in a tropical country and plan to travel to the United States in the winter, allow extra time to get warm clothes before the trip. The clothes may not be available in your country and delivery may take two to three weeks if ordering online.

Similarly, if you come from a humid country, make sure that you bring heavy-duty moisturizer and lip balm—it is annoying to have itchy skin and cracked lips when you take the exam.

Visit the Test Center You should try your best to visit the Prometric center in advance. There are two purposes for this pretrip:

1. To record the traveling time from home or hotel to the testing center. It is best to schedule your trip at the same time of the day to account for similar traffic conditions.
2. To visualize the experience on the exam day. This rehearsal can help reduce one of the many uncertainties that you will encounter on exam day and help you be psychologically well prepared.

Do Not Worry about Office Work It is important to keep your mind focused on the exam. I understand it is difficult to completely detach from your work with your BlackBerry and iPhone around, but try to convince your colleagues that you will be inaccessible for a couple of days. Your firm will survive without you.

Tell Yourself You Are Ready Spend the afternoon working on a few practice questions, do something relaxing such as a light dinner with friends or watching TV. Tell yourself you are ready, and go to bed early.

What to Bring on Exam Day

Here are the three items that you must bring to the exam site for both the U.S. and international Prometric centers:

1. NTS
2. Primary identification
3. Secondary identification

The NTS is a very important document: This slip is your admission ticket; it also contains information such as the exam ID for logging in to your preregistered sections.

The primary identification must include a photo and signature. Driver's licenses and passports are the most common examples. The secondary identification may not include a photo but must have the signature. Examples include an additional government-issued identification, ATM card, and debit/credit card. Note that social security cards, U.S. permanent residency cards (green cards), employee IDs, and student ID cards are not accepted as identification.

If you come from a non-English speaking country, the best primary identification is your passport. Check whether your passport includes a presentation of your name in English. Also, if your passport does not require a signature, you must present a secondary identification with signature.

If your name on the passport is not written in English or no signature is required, you may apply for a NASBA Candidate Identification Card by emailing nasbastore@nasba.org.

Note

1. If you register the sections one at a time and have multiple NTS, you must double-check to bring the correct NTS with you.
2. The identifications should be valid, unaltered, and undamaged and the name on the NTS should be spelled exactly the same as those on both identifications.

What You Might Bring to the Testing Center   Consider bringing the following items on the exam day:

- Jacket—In case the air conditioning is very strong. You can wear the jacket in the testing room (if so, you must wear it at all times) or keep it in the storage locker.
- Earplugs with no string attached—All exam takers are required to keep quiet but ear plugs are allowed if you need absolute silence.

- Flash card or final review notes—In reality you will not have time for more studying but for many candidates it brings some comfort to have a small stack of notes around.
- Wallet.
- Mobile phone.
- Umbrella.
- Aspirin or pain reliever—In case you have a severe headache, you can take it during the break.
- Medications if necessary.
- Small water bottle—Mostly for a sip of refreshment before and after the exam.
- Favorite snack—To congratulate yourself after the exam!

Other than the earplugs and jacket, all items listed above must be kept in the storage locker.

What *Not* to Bring   Although it is obvious that items such as cigarettes and cameras will not be allowed, the following items are also prohibited in the testing room (but can be stored in storage locker):

- Calculator
- Container of any kind (including eyeglass cases)
- Earphone, headset, or audio earmuff
- Hat, except head coverings worn for religious reasons
- Nonprescription sunglasses
- Paper
- Pendant necklace or large earrings
- Stationery such as pen, pencil, eraser, and ruler
- Watch

What to Expect at the Prometric Center

Imagine it is exam day today.

Your exam is scheduled for 10 A.M. and your appointment time is 9:30 A.M. You arrive at the test center 30 minutes early as suggested, at 9 A.M. There are three people waiting in line before you. The rest are sitting and reviewing study notes for lawyers, nurses, and all sorts of different professions.

The waiting takes longer than expected because the candidate before you forgot to sign his ATM card and it takes him a lot of time to dig out another valid ID.

Fifteen minutes later, the administrator greets you and asks for the identifications. You hand over the NTS, driver's license, and credit card. The staff scans the IDs and takes a digital photograph of you for the record. After signing in, you are given a key for the storage locker where you can put all your belongings. The locker is small and you are glad to have brought a small backpack instead of the big tote. You also take the time to take a sip of water and go to the washroom.

At 9:30 A.M., you are asked to enter the testing room. The staff scans each candidate with a handheld metal detector wand and collects a fingerprint copy. You are given a fine-point marker and two pieces of note cards to write notes, and you are then escorted to the workstation. After entering the launch code, the monitor shows a series of introductory screens, which you need to respond to and complete within 10 minutes.

You proceed to take the exam. After you are done, there is an online survey that you can fill in. Then, you return the marker and note cards, sign the test center log book, and receive a Confirmation of Attendance with contact details should you have questions after the exam.

The Introductory Examination Screens

The 30 minutes between the appointment time and scheduled exam time is required for candidates to log in to the computer, read the introductory screens before the exam, and complete a survey after the exam. This is considered part of the test and you must arrive before the appointment time instead of right at the exam time.

At the same time, this 30 minutes is separate from the exam itself: If you complete each step quickly and have extra time, it will *not* be counted as additional time for the examination.

Taking the Break . . . Or Not

I do not recommend it, but you are allowed to take breaks between the testlets. Be prepared to go through the procedure of being scanned and fingerprinted when leaving and reentering the testing room. The clock will keep running between the breaks so make sure you use the break wisely. Breaks that last more than 10 minutes will be reported to the state board.

What to Expect after the Exam

First of all, take a good break. You deserve it! Then, thank your loved ones—a cheerful phone call to let them know you are done (for now, at least) or handwritten note on a pretty card—their support is crucial to maintaining your sanity throughout the CPA journey.

On the other end, your exam responses are forwarded to the AICPA for scoring. When the score is available, it is forwarded to NASBA to match the scores to individual candidates. NASBA then forwards the scores to boards of accountancy for approval and subsequent release to candidates.

Here is the timetable of the score release:

- Day 1–20: 11 business days following day 20 of the testing window
- Day 21–45: six business days following day 45 of the testing window
- Day 46–close of window: six business days following the close of the testing window
- After close of window: six business days after receiving all scoring data for the testing window

Note that scores are not released in any specific order and candidates who take the exam at the same time may receive the score at different times.

Are You Ready?

Now that we have a good idea of what is ahead, let us get the planning done!

CHAPTER

Creating a Study Plan

I know you are eager to start studying for the exam, but there is something you must do before that. That's right—a good, workable study plan.

But I Can't Afford to Plan. I Am So Busy!

Your work and family commitments will never let you set aside a fixed time to study, which makes planning anything irrelevant, and I totally understand that. But this is precisely why you need a plan to make sure you do not fall behind; and in case you do, you can catch up to complete the review before it is too late.

The Plan Keeps You Organized

As an accountant, you understand how important audit planning is for the whole audit exercise. You should therefore create an equally rigorous plan for your own CPA project.

The Plan Identifies Extra Time for Study

As you draft your plan, you will be able to identify 15 minutes here and a half hour there that you can effectively use for studying every day. This could be the idle time on the commute, or the lunch hour when you chitchat with your colleagues.

I am not saying that you should squeeze out every minute for studying and drive yourself crazy, but you can certainly review practice questions during lunch from Monday to Thursday and hang out with your colleagues on Friday. The exam preparation requires some sacrifices and a study plan will help you minimize these sacrifices by effectively utilizing the time you have.

The Plan Builds Up Confidence

It feels great when you can visualize your progress—as you cross out the topics you have mastered, it builds up confidence, which makes studying less tedious and more efficient. I urge you to take a pen and paper right now and we'll work on the plan together!

Step 1: Aim to Complete the Exam within One Year

The examiners give you an 18-month window: you must pass the four sections of the CPA exam within 1.5 years. I generally recommend that you aim for completion within one year. Why?

- You have six months of buffer in case of a retake, or when more important things in life force you to take a short break.
- The four sections are connected in some way. There are synergies if you take them within a short period of time. This is the case for Financial Accounting and Reporting (FAR) and Audit and Attestation (AUD), and to a lesser extent Business Environment and Concepts (BEC).

Step 2: Settle on the Sequence

I recommend that you take on the toughest exam first, because you want to get done with the biggest beast before the 18-month clock starts to tick. The majority of my readers agree that FAR is the toughest—not necessarily because it is the most difficult, but that it covers a huge amount of material.

Then I suggest that you take AUD next. In my opinion, FAR and AUD should always go together (AUD following FAR) because there are many references to FAR in the AUD exam.

Then, for BEC or REG, I am quite neutral. I would say BEC is shorter and easier for most candidates, and it could be somewhat related to FAR. You can consider scheduling BEC at the busiest time of the year such as the tax season, the audit season, or your children's exam periods.

The question is, which one is easier? Everyone has different strengths—for example, a tax accountant would find REG a breeze while I personally found REG to be very difficult. I thought AUD was relatively straightforward but it has the lowest passing rate among the four sections in 2012.

How about Taking Multiple Sections at the Same Time?

There are six to seven testing windows in each 18-month period, which means you only have two to three chances for retakes or postponing of exams due to work, family, or health reasons. If you can spare sufficient time to prepare for two sections within the same testing window, give it a try.

If you are an international candidate who will travel far to take the exam, I highly recommend that you take two if not more sections in one go. I took four sections two days in a row to save travel and accommodation costs. This is an extreme case and not everyone can afford the commitment to prepare for the exam so intensely. It is more important for you to know the reason behind the suggested sequence of the exams and make your own decision.

Step 3: Estimate the Time Required for Study

There are different ways you can tackle the study materials, and in many cases, it depends on how much time you have. I present the following four plans as an illustration of how you can customize your own study program.

Plan A: Six Hours per Day from Monday to Saturday

- Number of hours per week: 36

Candidates who can spend six hours per day every day except Sunday are likely those who do not work full time and have minimal family commitment. They can be recent graduates who take a year off to study for the CPA exam, freelancers, and housewives, many of whom hold a spouse visa, are barred from working in the United States, and so have plenty of time to study.

If you have a good knowledge of accounting either as a major in this subject or a professional with prior accounting experience, you should aim to complete the exam within six to nine months.

Unlike other candidates, you do not need to learn the theory and should instead skim through the review book and dive into the practice questions as soon as possible.

If you are relatively new to accounting, then you might need the standard 12 months to complete the whole process.

Plan B: Three Hours on Weekdays; Six Hours on Weekends

- Number of hours per week: 27

This plan is suitable for those with a part-time job or a more relaxed full-time work schedule with some family commitment, such as having school-age children.

With almost 30 hours per week dedicated to study, you are lucky compared to many other candidates. However, allocating six work hours on weekends means less time to spend with your children, and fewer lunches and dinners with friends. You may need extra help from an understanding spouse, parents, helpful neighbors, or part-time nannies to make life easier for you and your family.

Plan C: Eight Hours on Both Weekend Days Every Week

- Number of hours per week: 16

This plan is applicable to those with a busy working lifestyle but little family commitment. This could be your plan if you work in public accounting firms or a demanding corporate environment but without children, elderly, or other dependents to take care of.

I suggest that you allocate at least one unscheduled week every four to five weeks so you can get out to visit friends, run errands, or catch up if you are behind your study schedule.

I used Plan C myself. Eight hours of studying means full-time study with time only for cooking a simple meal, eating, and washing the dishes afterward. Do not expect to have time to watch TV, to chat with friends on the phone, or to hang out with them, but you can arrange these activities on Friday nights.

Plan D: Two Hours Every Day Except Sunday or Family Day

- Number of hours per week: 12

This is a plan for courageous candidates: the busy working mothers and fathers who against all odds pass the CPA exam with full-time work and family commitments.

I strongly encourage you to find reliable help in advance to make your plan work, to avoid your precious two hours being eaten up by young children getting sick, overtime at work, and many factors that are out of your control. You can consider going to work two hours early or staying two hours after work to make sure you have time and space of your own to maximize these two hours. Most important, schedule some breaks in between. You will need that!

Step 4: Plan to Complete Each Section in One Quarter

Allocating three months for each section is a good way to start, but you might want to adjust the time based on your own strengths and weaknesses in respective areas. For most candidates, FAR and REG take up more study time, while BEC generally takes less.

Your next question will likely be . . .

How Long Do I Need to Study for Each Section?

A 38-year-old financial controller with three young children requires a much longer study program than a 23-year-old new graduate, given the work and family commitment as well as the depreciation of "book smartness" after graduation.

Here is the average of the number of hours suggested by major CPA review course providers:

- FAR: 120–160 hours
- AUD: 60–90 hours
- REG: 90–110 hours
- BEC: 60–80 hours
- Total: 330–440 hours

Note that there are people who studied (and passed) with one week of study, while some logged 400 studying hours and still failed . . . you need to adjust the program based on your own strengths and weaknesses.

FAR   For 120 to 160 hours of required study time, this translates into:

- Plan A: 3.3–4.4 weeks
- Plan B: 4.4–5.9 weeks
- Plan C: 7.5–10.0 weeks
- Plan D: 10.0–13.3 weeks

What does this mean? If you take Plan A—six hours per day and six days per week (36 hours per week)—then you can expect to complete the studying of FAR in 3.3 to 4.4 weeks.

FAR covers what an accounting major should have learned during his four to five years of study. Therefore, expect a huge volume of coursework.

If you are familiar with financial accounting, you can skip most of the review process and start working on the practice questions directly. For those taking Plan A, it is possible to complete the studying within one month. Even if you take Plan D, you can comfortably cover all materials within a quarter.

However, if your study or work does not involve financial accounting, then expect to spend a fair amount of time understanding the theory and calculations before the review process. In this case, focus only on FAR and allocate more time per week to study (at least Plan B if Plan A is not possible). Otherwise, allocate more than three months for studying to avoid stressing out with looming deadlines.

TIP

Do not prepare for a single section for more than six months. It will bore you to tears and your efficiency will go seriously downhill toward the end of the period.

AUD   For 60 to 90 hours of required studying, this translates into:

- Plan A: 1.7–2.5 weeks
- Plan B: 2.2–3.3 weeks
- Plan C: 3.8–5.6 weeks
- Plan D: 5.0–7.5 weeks

AUD is relatively straightforward but requires more memoriza-tion instead of calculation. If your work actively involves auditing or if you have a good memory, you should be able to go through all study materials within three months no matter which plan you use. You can consider allocating more time to FAR and less to AUD.

AUD questions are based on U.S. generally accepted auditing standards (GAAS). International candidates may need extra time to adjust to the differences between auditing standards in the United States and in your country.

REG   For 90 to 110 hours of required studying time, this translates into:

- Plan A: 2.5–3.1 weeks
- Plan B: 3.3–4.1 weeks
- Plan C: 5.6–6.9 weeks
- Plan D: 7.5–9.2 weeks

REG tests business law, business ethics, and taxation. The required study time is highly dependent on your expertise (or lack of) in this area. You can complete studying in one month if you can skip the review and work directly on the practice questions; or as long as four months if you start from scratch.

International candidates can assume that REG is the most dif-ficult section because U.S. taxation is likely more complicated than the system used in your own country. Add at least two additional weeks to the above in your study plan.

BEC   For 60 to 80 hours of required study time, this translates into:

- Plan A: 1.7–2.2 weeks
- Plan B: 2.2–3.0 weeks
- Plan C: 3.8–5.0 weeks
- Plan D: 5.0–6.7 weeks

BEC covers many miscellaneous topics in business but each topic is manageable. Therefore, for most candidates this is considered the easiest and shortest section.

Although you should never underestimate any section, you can expect to complete studying in one to two months and therefore can spare the extra time for FAR or REG.

Business topics do not follow specific standards. International candidates do not need to allocate extra time for this section.

Step 5: Write It Down!

Your study program does not work if you just think about it in your head. Get a pen and a piece of paper now so we can go through creating a study plan together.

Step 1. Make a Realistic Estimate of Your Time Commitment

First of all, determine the number of hours you are able to take out from your normal life for this exam every week, and see which plan (A, B, C, or D) is the most applicable. Then, based on the plan, you can estimate the total length of study time, which should fall somewhere between 6 and 12 months.

Step 2. Select a CPA Review Course

You may want to settle on a specific CPA review material or course so you can flip through the content and make a more accurate estimate of the time required to study or review the material.

A number of CPA review course providers include an online study planner in the package. The tool is handy and can greatly facilitate your planning process. We discuss how you can identify the most suitable CPA review course in Chapter 7, "Study Tips and Exam-Taking Strategies."

Step 3. Display the Plan at a Prominent Place

I highly recommend that you print out your study plan and put it up on a wall next to your desk. It helps to build your confidence as you cross out the topics you have mastered, and confidence will greatly increase your chance of passing success.

Note

If you have any good ideas for creating study plans, or if you have awesome plans to share, drop me a note on my Facebook page: www.facebook.com/ipassthecpaexam.

How to Become More Efficient and Effective

As an aspiring CPA, you probably have gone through years of studying and have figured out the most common ways to do this effectively. Therefore, I am not going to bore you with cliché advice. I hope the following suggestions give you fresh ideas to motivate yourself to success.

To find ways to study effectively, let us talk about factors that have prevented us from doing so. Exam takers all over the world are troubled by:

- Not having enough time to study.
- Stressing out.
- Seeing little progress despite hard work.

To solve these problems, I show you how to:

- Create 25 hours in a day.
- Transform your stress into strength.
- Analyze your mistakes and make them your friends.

Create 25 Hours in a Day

In other words, how do you create additional time previously thought impossible? You can do this by:

- Identifying the time that has been spent unproductively.
- Supercharging yourself and make your 24 hours worth 25 hours or more.

Create More Productive Time

Trick Yourself into Getting Up Early   Try getting up an hour or two early to study. I am sure you have given this a thought but it is difficult to keep up. Here is the trick: If you manage to force yourself to get up and stay awake for five seconds, you won't fall back and snooze away. Here are three suggestions that work for me:

1. Prepare a wet towel on the bedside table the night before, and throw it on your face when you hear the alarm clock.
2. Place your favorite snack on the bedside table, and only allow yourself to eat if you leave the bed.
3. Place your alarm clock on the other side of the room.

Getting up early will be less miserable once you make it a habit.

Delegate. Outsource. Find a Helping Hand   One of the best ways to create more time is to have someone else perform tasks. You can delegate office work to your subordinates and household chores to your spouse and older children. It is worth the time planning and showing them how to take on the new responsibility, and making it a win-win situation. If this is not possible, you can outsource the work by asking for temporary help from parents, relatives, and neighbors, or by hiring a nanny or a helper for a few months.

Prioritize Based on the Long-Term Goals of Your Life   Finding extra time for studying means less time for activities you have been enjoying. If you think you absolutely must watch this TV episode, think about what it means to you 10 years from now. Does it make a difference to your life and your career?

Are there other activities that you can skip or postpone for similar reasons? You can create much more study time if you prioritize based on your long-term goals instead of short-term enjoyment.

Stop Being a Perfectionist   This is a common trait among accountants. Our work demands us to be perfectionists, and sometimes we forget that in real life, this is not necessary and could be impossible to achieve.

Apply the 80/20 rule—80 percent of results come from the first 20 percent of your effort. Put it another way: If you insist on getting 100 percent of the result, you need to put in an additional 80 percent of the effort (i.e., four times of the first 20 percent effort) to make it happen. Can you imagine how much time you can save by letting go and not striving for perfection?

Plan before You Act   Creating a plan takes time, effort, and is against human nature (I just want to do what I feel like doing!), but spending a few hours now will save you days if not weeks of work later. A good plan makes you study when you want to slack off, and keeps you on the right track when you drift off to work on something else. A plan is especially important if you don't have a tutor for your CPA exam study.

Pick the Right Tools   This means getting the best CPA review materials based on your background, budget, and learning style. The book or the course should be up-to-date (latest version) so you don't lose unnecessary points due to outdated materials.

This also means getting or borrowing a computer that supports online test preparation software, a well-designed chair that you can sit on comfortably for hours, and sufficient lighting to make your room a pleasant place to study. Getting the right tools helps you achieve more with less time, money, and effort.

Be Productive While You Wait   In Chapter 5, "Creating a Study Plan," we discussed how we can create a plan by reviewing your daily schedule and allocating time for the study. At the same time, you also need to identify pockets of idle time that you have every day, such as the waiting time during the commute, or when you wait for a meeting to start, or when you pick up the kids from school.

The idle time can be as long as an hour or as short as a few minutes, so you need to be creative and find the best way to utilize it. When I studied for my own exam years ago, I had my own hand-written flash cards with me everywhere. I still recommend the good old flash cards, but you have many more choices now ranging from audio reviews to mobile applications on your handheld devices.

A reader told me how she is a classic soccer mom who spends a lot of time taking her children to various activities. During her exam preparation, it was not possible to read the notes and drive at the same time, so she tried the audio review. She managed to skip all the reading and go straight to the practice problems.

Combine Family Time and Study Time   Writing this book made me experience the intensity and stress similar to what you are facing for the CPA exam. Therefore, I looked for new ways to create more time without sacrificing too much of what I need to do as a mother. I have done these activities with my children with great success. If you are a parent, you might want to give them a try.

I have a seven-year-old daughter and four-year-old son. Delegation is the first thing in mind: I asked my daughter to help little brother with schoolwork (drawing lines, counting numbers, and learning shapes) and reading to him every night. She was proud of mom's new role as an author and was eager to help. They spent more time drawing and reading together instead of fighting and shouting.

I needed to spend Saturday mornings in a library for a quiet and peaceful place to work. I brought my daughter along so she could enjoy reading books beside me. My son cannot read books on his own, so I enrolled him in a soccer class and my husband took him there and kept him busy.

For quality time with my son, I got him a series of audio books and he enjoyed listening and flipping the pages himself. He was happy to leave me alone as long as I stayed in the same room. I also taught him to take a shower himself and he was thrilled to learn a new skill. I took the laptop in the bathroom so I could write and watch him at the same time.

I am still looking for creative ways to combine family and work. If you have other good ideas, it would be great to share notes!

Optimizing versus Maximizing Your Study Effort

Most candidates focus on finding more time to study. As a smart candidate you can also consider how to optimize your study effort.

In the CPA exam, you need a score of 75 to pass, not 100. Therefore, instead of aiming to pass with flying colors, you can target to study enough to pass the exam. This is easier said than done: How can anyone draw a line? A rule of thumb is to attain 80 to 85 percent accuracy on your practice test questions. You can also read through 100 percent of the review materials and be reasonably confident in 80 to 85 percent of the topics, including the heavily tested areas.

In Chapter 7, "Study Tips and Exam-Taking Strategies," you will find a unique study methodology known as the *reverse adaptive method* that asks you to skip reviewing the materials altogether. For this you need to aim for an eventual 100 percent accuracy on the multiple-choice questions. Spend the time exploring various suggestions and customize a strategy based on your own learning style.

Create a More Productive Mind

Seek Privacy   Many of us get less stressed and more productive in a quiet, peaceful place all by ourselves. Try studying at the library, a park early in the morning, or the office after work so you can distance yourself from the kids, dogs, email, phone, dryer, vacuum cleaner, and all sorts of noise in your life.

Clear the Clutter   No time to clear the mess in your room and office? This is worth investing your time on. A pleasant, stress-free living space cheers you up and keeps you focused, organized, and efficient.

Use Visual Reminders   Do you know how many brain cells we kill every day trying to remember mundane details? Put your mind at rest by writing them down in one place.

Do Not Worry about the Uncontrollable   Will questions on government accounting show up in the exam? What if I have never seen the format in the task-based simulations? What if I get sick before the exam? What if . . . ?

Don't worry about things you have no control over, and stop making up scenarios and hurting your confidence. Take action on what you have control over: Select the most suitable review course, draft a workable study plan, complete the practice questions, master the simulations, pack for your trip, and take the exam with confidence— take charge of your goal and your life one step at a time.

Stop Complaining and Stay Positive   We go through many ups and downs during studying. On grumpy days we may want to complain about everything from the state boards to the dry cleaning. But complaints drag us down and distract us from our studies. Complaints also foster a dangerous habit of putting the blame on someone else instead of taking responsibility. Try your best to stay positive by reviewing the road map of your goals, appreciating your family and friends, sticking motivating quotes on the wall, and simply by smiling more.

Note

Check out this blog! These tips are partly inspired by Marc's blog on productive living. Visit Marc and Angel Hack Life at www.marcandangel.com.

Transform Your Stress into Strength

It is inevitable that you will get anxious, nervous, and restless during the CPA exam preparation. Therefore, it is important to learn how to control the stress level and better yet, transform this negative force into positive energy. Before you take on this fight, you have to understand the enemy. Where exactly does your stress come from?

Stress from the Exam

The Fear of Not Having Enough Time to Study   I cannot emphasize more about the importance of creating a study plan. If you can only allocate two hours per day for studying, then you can allow sufficient preparation time by scheduling the test in four months' time instead of two to three months and getting all stressed out. This is the best and simplest way to solve this common issue.

The Fear of Underpreparing for the Exam   There are parts of the exam for which you can never fully prepare, but every candidate is in the same situation and you are in no way worse off than anyone else. If you pick good study materials, work on most of the practice questions, and learn from your mistakes, you can be well prepared. Tell yourself that you are well prepared—confidence is a big part toward passing success.

The Fear of Failing the Exam   We discussed how we can avoid worrying about something that is out of our control—and this is one of them. Turn your fear into action, do what you can in the preparation, face the challenge, and wait for the result.

Stress from the Family

Many candidates did not realize the level of stress they get from the family. It can be a combination of:

- The guilt of not spending enough time with the family
- The fear of not getting their support and understanding
- The anxiety of letting them down if you fail

The bottom line is, your family cares, and they want to help. Instead of alienating yourself and creating issues with the isolation, you should embrace their kindness and make good use of their support to achieve your goal.

Bring Them in as Valuable Contributors in Your Planning Phase   It is best if you can draw them in at the very beginning of exam preparation. I recommend that you hold a family meeting to explain how important the CPA qualification is to you, and how the family can help you achieve this goal by mapping out a study plan together.

You can then discuss how you want to allocate time for your study, and brainstorm ideas on how to get this done. Your family members will most likely volunteer to share some of your household chores, and they may have other interesting ideas to help create more time for your studies.

During the brainstorming session, your family members will have a better understanding of the CPA exam and how much you need to go through to get this done.

Enroll Your Family as Study Buddies   Now that you have created a road map as team members, why not ask them to be your study buddies? I do not mean enrolling them in accounting classes, but having them around to cheer you up would be a great way to start.

I considered my daughter an important "project buddy" when I wrote this book. One day, I woke up early to work on the book when the rest of the family was still sleeping—or so I thought. My daughter came in, holding a tray with a piece of sandwich and a glass of milk, and leaned forward, "You are on page 88? Good job!" Is she not the best buddy I could ever find?

My mother-in-law cannot read English and had little idea about what I was writing, but she stopped by every Sunday to prepare dinner and wash the dishes for us. My husband is the managing director at his firm but he made an effort to come home earlier or work at home to take care of the kids.

Stay Committed to Get the Respect   Now that you are asking your family to sacrifice in some way or another, make sure that you are committed to the exam. It is not cool to be seen checking your Facebook when you are supposed to be working on the practice questions. When you make plans to get up early but end up snoozing away, it is hard to get the respect and support from the rest of your family.

Lower Your Expectations   In the coming months, you will be contributing less as a member of the family. It is understandable that you should expect less. Your wife has not ironed your shirt? Chances are that you forgot to vacuum the floor for a month now that you spend day and night studying. Your child did not do well on his test? You do not know if you can pass your own exam!

Be Considerate of Their Reactions   There will be days when your family looks uncaring when you crave for their support. As you go through your own emotional ups and downs during the preparation, your family will inevitably be affected. If they look uncaring or even frustrated, it is totally understandable. Similarly, do not get stressed out because you do not want to let them down in case you fail. After all, it is your exam and it is pursued for your own achievement.

Show Your Appreciation from Time to Time   Be thankful when family members make the effort to help you. It can be as simple as a cheerful thank you, a hug, and a smile. It can also be something thoughtful. For example, when you draft the study plan, you can suggest how the family can do something fun together after the exam.

A pleasant surprise would be nice, too. I planned to send a handwritten thank you card to each member of my family after finishing this book. What can you do after your exam?

Stress from Friends

Taking the CPA exam means less personal time, including time with your friends. You may worry about losing touch, misunderstanding, and how your friends may think of you in case you fail the exam.

Share Your Plans   Your friends may not be accountants and they may have difficulty understanding the importance of the CPA exam. For close friends with whom you meet regularly, you should spend the time and tell them about your goals and why this is important for you and your career. Unlike your family, there will be fewer opportunities for them to be helpful but you can certainly brainstorm for ideas. For friends you do not see regularly, choose to take no action until you find a time to meet with them, which will likely be after the exam.

Announce Your Plan on Social Media   If you do want to keep all your friends updated, the most efficient way is to announce your plan on Facebook or other social media. Tell them that you need to prepare for a big professional exam and it will be harder to get in touch in the next few months.

I am too busy to maintain an active personal social media account, but I connect with my friends by sending out an annual e-newsletter. You may consider doing something similar by emailing a personal note to tell your friends about your latest CPA "project."

Be Considerate and Show Gratitude   If you are contributing less to the friendship, you can expect less from the friendship during this time. Do not expect your friends to call you every day to cheer you up; do not overreact if they do not seem to care. In most cases, your friends may simply want to leave you alone so you can focus on your studies. They will be happy to hang out with you again once you are ready, after the exam.

A few close friends may bend over backward and care about you as much as your family does. Be expressively thankful to these buddies and put them back on your priority list immediately after the exam.

Stress from Your Boss and Colleagues

The stress from the workplace can be quite complicated. If you work in public accounting and you are expected to work toward your CPA, then the stress comes from the expectation of your supervisor and peer pressure from your colleagues, who may also be taking the exam around the same time. However, if you do not work in public accounting, your stress may come from a completely different source. We discuss both situations next.

Expectation from Supervisor   If you work in public accounting, your supervisor will most likely be a CPA. Having such a supervisor can be a double-edge sword: On one hand, he should fully understand the stress you are going through and may even lend a hand by assigning fewer work projects or allowing you to take paid leaves for the study. On the other hand, he may give you a challenge to pass the four sections on the first try, or to complete the exam within certain number of months, all of which will add unnecessary pressure on your part.

My suggestion is to take it easy. You take the exam for your own career development, not for the boss, not for the firm. If you meet the challenge, take it as a bonus, but if you do not, it is completely fine.

For the same reason, do not expect your supervisor to give you less work because you are going through the exam.

Peer Pressure from Colleagues   You may be taking the exam around the same time as colleagues. They can be your study buddies, supporting each other and passing the exam together.

In a less perfect and probably more realistic scenario, this situation could be a competition in disguise—what will happen if everyone but you passes the exam? Bosses tend to make unhelpful comments on how the CPA exam has become so much easier since his time, and annoying colleagues may brag how that "CPA thing" is a piece of cake. There is little truth in these claims. Stay calm, stick to your own plan, and work toward your own success.

Pressure from the Management   You are an experienced financial controller who never had the time to take the CPA exam. The day comes when you receive an ultimatum from your management to get the CPA within six months, or out. I got many panic emails from readers in this situation.

The advice is to get your CPA qualifications as soon as possible. If this advice comes too late, you have to fight off the pressure and take advantage of your practical experience to complete the exam within the deadline. We go over the study tips and exam-taking strategies in the next chapter.

Unexpected Reactions from Coworkers   If you are currently not working in the accounting field, your coworkers may wonder why you need to put yourself through this hardship. Some may not even know what a Certified Public Accountant (CPA) is. In this case, do not expect your coworkers to be understanding or even expect them to share your workload. You must find additional time outside of work for studying and get emotional support from your family and friends instead.

If you do work in accounting but your supervisor is not a CPA, be careful. This person may see you as a threat instead of a more valuable member of the firm. Keep a low profile and study at home instead of making your exam preparation the talk of the day in the office and potentially embarrassing your boss.

Let's Move On!

Now that we are all efficient and effective, let's go straight to the studying strategies for the exam.

CHAPTER

7

Study Tips and Exam-Taking Strategies

In this chapter we go through the tips on the preparation for the exam as well as the strategies on how to optimize your performance on the exam day.

Study Tips

Here are some suggestions for how you can prepare for the exam more effectively and efficiently.

Selecting the Most Suitable versus the "Best" CPA Review Course

Many readers ask me for recommendations of the "best" CPA review courses. I do not think there exists a review product that is the absolute best, but you can find one that is most suitable based on your background, budget, time commitment, self-study versus live class preference, and learning style.

Your Educational Background The intensity of the review materials largely depends on your own background.

If you recently graduated from an accounting program in the United States, there is probably no need to purchase a fully guided CPA review course. It can be boring for you to go over the concepts again and waste valuable time. Instead, get yourself a stack of summary notes and jump directly to the practice questions. The *Wiley Focused Notes* and *Wiley CPA Test Bank* are among the best choices in this category.

If you have been out of school for a while or you studied accounting outside the United States, then it makes more sense to get a guided review course. You can review certain sections of the exam (such as Financial Accounting and Reporting [FAR] and Business Environment and Concepts [BEC]) relatively quickly and move on to the practice questions.

If you are not an accounting major and your job does not involve accounting, then you must get a guided review course with comprehensive lecture notes, and preferably one that allows you to ask questions online or by phone. The suggested 300 to 400 hours of review time outlined in Chapter 6 assumes that you know accounting. Allocate additional time if you need to learn new material.

Budget Budget is an important consideration for recent graduates with student loans and international candidates who will be spending a substantial amount in travel and accommodation expenses.

First of all, decide whether you want to get the books or a guided review course. Review courses offer an integrated approach that is a more comprehensive way of learning for most candidates.

Although I do not believe that the most expensive must mean the best, I refrain from selecting review courses that cost less than $1,000. It takes considerable resources to hire good-quality teaching staff to update the materials and record the lecture on a yearly basis, and provide adequate customer support at the same time. A course that costs less may not have the resources to keep up with this standard. You also want to avoid review providers who compete on price and not the quality of the product.

If you cannot afford $1,000 for the course, I would suggest you go for the CPA review books. Many candidates pass the CPA exam with these books alone. We talk about how you can make full use of the review books later in the chapter.

In my opinion, the one must-have learning tool is the online test preparation software. The CPA exam is 100 percent computerized and you put yourself at a disadvantage if you do not have the chance to practice answering questions in this particular format. If you have the budget to choose only the book and the software, pick the software.

What I like about the test preparation software is that it allows me to practice in a format that is similar to that of the setting in the test center. With the prep book I have, I am only able to practice in paper format. I also use the free CPA questions online but it is not in a format similar to that of the CPA exam and it does not provide detailed feedback.

Another great function of the test bank is its customization. As I am taking five online classes this semester, searching for a full time job, working part time, and taking care of my family, being able to customize the practice session by number of questions is very useful. I can tailor the length of the practice session based on my available time. That will motivate me to study even if I have only 30 minutes. I believe that the test prep software would be a great resource for my CPA preparation and will greatly increase my chance of passing.

—Ying

Time Commitment   Do you have a deadline to pass the CPA exam? If so, you have to pick a CPA review course or material that closely matches your study plan. Some review courses focus on teaching solid concepts, but expect to spend a lot more time on your studies. Others divide the courses into bite-size lectures and it is easier for busy professionals to squeeze in a minicourse or two during their commute or lunch time.

If your work requires a lot of traveling, you might want to pick a self-study course versus a live class to avoid the hassle of frequent rescheduling of classes.

Self-Study versus Live Class Preference   I personally prefer the self-study course style because it saves travel time and I can study in my pajamas in the comfort of my home. I can also choose to rewatch the video as many times as I like if the concept is new to me.

Theoretically, in live classes you can identify study buddies and the lecturer can help monitor your progress. From my own experience, rarely did students talk to each other in class. They were either too tired or wanted to rush home and continue to study. The teaching assistant did little to motivate us—all he did was check our names off the attendance list. He did not seem to care whether we attended the class and whether we passed or failed the exam.

I am sure you can find lecturers who are much more responsible and caring. If you want to give live classes a try, ask around for the reputation of the lecturer before signing up.

Learning Style   Another important consideration is the teaching style that works best for you. If you are a visual learner, it is much easier to learn by watching a professor's lecture on a video or in person. Audio review may not work for you in this case. For analytics gurus, you may appreciate review courses with sophisticated diagnostic analysis of your performance and progress, while some may prefer the good old book where you can scribble notes in the margins.

Some of you may appreciate the sleek audiovisual presentations with animated graph and charts, while others may prefer the old-school approach, watching the professors explain a concept by writing on the white board and throwing in a tip or two in the conversation.

The best way to learn about the various teaching styles is to watch the demo videos available in most of the CPA review providers' websites. Listen long enough and determine whether the lecturer is too boring or too agitated, too slow or too fast, no value-add (e.g., reading from the lecture notes) or helpful and motivational. Any CPA review course is expensive—it is worth spending the time to pick the best for your needs.

> **Note**
>
> You can check out my analysis of the 10 major CPA review courses here: http://ipassthecpaexam.com/cpa-exam-review-courses/.

How to Pass with CPA Review Books Alone

I understand that the examination fee is a huge amount to pay, on top of other necessities such as the CPA review materials. If you can only afford to purchase a set of CPA review books or the test preparation software, here are my suggestions on how you can make the best use of it.

Make Full Use of Each Multiple-Choice Question   Many candidates do not realize that the multiple-choice questions are much more than a practicing tool—they can be used as an integral part of your study.

We learn a concept by reading the theories, but we learn how to apply a concept by reading the examples. The explanations in the answers are the best examples you can find for each concept. Better yet, the three wrong answers in each multiple-choice question provide further examples on how the concepts should not be applied and therefore you are able to learn in different perspectives.

Prepare Your Own Summary Based on the Review Books   Another effective way with no additional cost is to make your own summary based on the CPA review books. You can do this by writing notes on flash cards or by reading and recording your own audio review.

Reading the concepts and presenting a summary version in a medium that works best for you is the most effective (and priceless) learning tool that you can get. It does take time to prepare but the preparation time is a good part of the learning process.

This method is especially useful for conceptual and memorization-oriented sections, such as Audit and Attestation (AUD), and to a lesser extent, BEC and Regulation (REG). Give it a try and see if it works for you.

Never Use Outdated Review Materials   If you are on budget, I am sure that getting secondhand books crossed your mind. This is a great idea except that you should always only get the latest version. The most reputable review books are updated annually. Latest version means not more than one year old.

Studying based on outdated books puts you at a clear disadvantage compared to the rest of the candidates. If you get a score of 73, you will be haunted by the thought that if you used the latest version you would have gotten a 75, and this might well be the case. The risk of extra money and time for a retake does not justify the use of outdated review materials.

Reviewing versus Practicing: Finding the Right Balance

Reviewing is a passive activity; one can hardly stay focused when reading pages and pages of accounting concepts. Working on practice questions is an active activity; one has to understand the question and apply an accounting concept to come up with the answer.

In my opinion, review by reading is one of the least effective ways of learning. Your mind is not actively engaged and you can easily spend hours without learning anything. I still remember the first week when I read the lecture notes over and over and thought I got the concepts right. It was not until I tried the practice questions and got half of them wrong that I realized it was not going to work.

I am not saying that you should stop reviewing the lecture notes. They could be important especially if the concepts are new to you. There are, however, smarter ways of reading.

Read and Write Notes at the Same Time   We discuss how I benefited from writing summaries on flash cards later in this chapter. If preparing flash cards is not your style, you can try scribbling some notes in the margin of the book (or on the lecture notes if you are viewing the video), or write down the formulas when calculations are involved. It helps to keep your mind active while you are reading.

Keep Reading Time Short   Reviewing the topics one at a time, or separating longer topics into shorter ones helps retention. You can work on practice questions between the topics or at least something else (such as taking a short break) so you do not keep reading for hours and hours.

Gradually Reduce Your Reading Time and Increase Your Practicing Time   In the first month of my own exam study, I spent half the time reviewing and writing my notes on flash cards and the other half on practice questions. Once the concepts started to sink in, I spent 100 percent of the time working on practice questions, reinforcing the concepts I learned by reading the explanation of the multiple-choice questions. At the end, I probably spent 80 percent of the time on actual practice and only 20 percent of the time reading and reviewing.

A Simple Trick That Greatly Helps Retention

One of the best decisions I made was to rewrite and summarize the lecture notes on flash cards. I tell you why I did it, and why it worked for me.

First of all, I am always a note-taking person, because the process helps me retain the materials, and it is more efficient for me to study notes written in my own style. The size of the cards forces me to divide the topics into small, manageable bits and this makes studying more flexible.

Most of the time, I viewed/listened to the lecture first and wrote my study notes at home right afterward. Sometimes, I listened to the lecture and took notes at the same time. It largely depended on whether the material was new to me.

I prepared notes on 3×5-inch flash cards so I could:

- Carry them around.
- Put each card away when I am confident I understand the materials. It is a great feeling when you see the stack getting thinner and thinner every day.

I never found the need to refer back to the original lecture notes. The volume of study material reduced significantly—the cards probably weighed a few hundred grams compared to the lecture notes, which weighed more than 10 pounds altogether.

Tips on Preparing Your Own Flash Cards   Write down only the concepts that you do not know. There is no time to relearn the things you know. It also defeats the purpose of preparing your own notes. I drew charts and images on the cards, and marked important concepts in different colors. Some readers draw mind maps for every major concept. Prepare your cards in the style that works best for you.

What If My Review Course Comes with Flash Cards?   You can flip through the cards, pick the ones relevant to your own needs, and write additional notes on them if necessary.

Studying on the Go   Now that everything is mobile, you can easily review the courses using an iPod/iPad, read the ebook on Kindle, as well as run CPA review apps on various handheld electronic devices.

Are Mnemonics Useful?

A number of CPA review courses have an interesting collection of mnemonics to help candidates memorize a list of keywords within a topic. Mnemonics are great for this purpose, but the CPA exam is much more than memorizing a bunch of lists. You need to understand the concepts behind the list and how they can apply to real life business situations.

Learn from Your Mistakes

Many of us also put too much emphasis on how much we did right. I know it feels good when you achieve a certain score in your test prep software, but the software's biggest value-add is its ability to track what you have done wrong. Once we learn from the mistakes, we have a much higher chance of getting the correct answer next time.

Step 1. Study the Explanation for Both Correct and Incorrect Answers   Identifying the wrong question is the first step of this exercise. The second step is to understand what you did wrong by reading the explanations for all the answers. Study the correct answer and learn the concept behind it; at the same time, you can also study the three incorrect answers and understand why they are wrong.

Step 2. Redo the Questions   Rework the incorrect questions. If you get the wrong answer again, it means that you have not understood how the concept is applied. It is worth the time to review this particular topic. If you answer correctly, make sure that you got it right for the right reason and not because you remember the answer is "C."

Step 3. Look for "Patterns"   Sometimes, you get the questions wrong even if you know the concept. That's right, you get tricked. Did you get misled by the same type of questions? Common "traps" include:

- Misreading the question (e.g., did not notice the "not" in the question).
- Getting confused with the answers.
- There are several correct answers. You pick the first one on the list instead of the best one on the list.

Once you identify a pattern, you can pay special attention when you see a similar type of question in the exam. This is especially applicable to conceptual and subjective questions common in AUD. I bet you can easily get back 5 to 10 points with this tactic.

The "Reverse Adaptive" Method   A reader suggested an intriguing way of using only the test preparation software with review books as reference. If I take another professional exam I will give it a try.

>   **Step 1**: For each topic, work on all multiple-choice questions. Expect to get many questions wrong. Mark the ones with wrong answers.

>   **Step 2**: Skim through the correct answers to make sure you got them right for the right reasons; for the wrong ones, take

time to study the concepts or how the calculation should be done. Refer to review books if necessary.

Step 3: Repeat Step 1 and 2 in other topics.

Step 4: A few days later, rework the wrong questions. Mark the ones done incorrectly. For these questions it is the second time you got the wrong answers. It is important to analyze the reason and aim to get all of them right in the next attempt.

Step 5: Work again on the questions you did wrong twice. Repeat this step until you achieve 100 percent accuracy.

The Pros   This is an excellent way to:

- Study using one of the most affordable options.
- Spend more time on practicing, which I believe is a more effective method.
- Learn from the mistakes.

The Cons   This methodology works best for those who have a good knowledge in the tested areas, for example, recent graduates of accounting programs. Tax professionals can use this method for REG but probably not FAR and AUD; vice versa for financial accountants and auditors.

Another drawback is that by working again on certain questions several times you tend to memorize the answers without the need to understand the questions. I do not think this is a big problem as long as you take the time to go through the reasoning even if you remember the answer.

Set Up a Mock Exam

It is a useful exercise to go through an almost-real exam experience by setting up a mock exam. Find a place that mimics the testing environment (a library would be a good choice) and set aside four hours for your "rehearsal." If you do not have sufficient time to work on all sections, pick FAR or REG because candidates tend to run out of time in these two sections.

Wear clothes that are similar to what you will wear on the exam day. Put away your watch, cell phone, calculators, water bottles, and other exam-prohibited items. It is also an excellent opportunity to test how long you can go without a toilet break. Once you go through this exercise, you will be psychologically well prepared to tackle the real exam.

When It Is Time to Switch to Plan B

If you have a hard time catching up to the study schedule, or an emergency comes up that ate up two weeks of valuable study time, it is time to switch to Plan B—the "cram mode."

Prioritize to Cover All Materials   Try your best to read over all the materials. For the CPA exam, knowing a little about everything is much better than knowing everything about a few things.

Start skimming through the topics in the following order:

- Your weak and heavily tested areas
- Your weak and lightly tested areas
- Your strong and heavily tested areas
- Your strong and lightly tested areas

Skip the Detail Review and Go Straight to Practice Questions   In cram mode you need to learn and practice at the same time. Take the time to read the explanation so you can learn about the application of the accounting concepts.

Cut Back the Sleep   This is the easiest way to create more study time. Rania, one of my favorite readers, shared her amazing story of completing the CPA exam in five months with two children and a full-time job:

> Hi Stephanie,
>
> Thank you for the great website and motivation you provide to CPA testers. I passed my CPA exams on the first try and I thought about sharing my story with you.
>
> I am an international candidate, with two kids and a full-time job. I started preparing for the CPA exam in June 2012 (self-study), sat for FAR (passed with 89) & AUD (passed with 78) in August 2012. I sat for REG (passed with 84) & BEC (passed with 80) early November 2012. Yes, 5 months of studying with full-time job & two kids, and I did it! How?
>
> With discipline, strong will, & faith in GOD. I used to teach my kids and help them do their school homework, cook, put them to bed at 7 pm and sleep afterwards. Wake up at 2 am and study

till 6 am. Leave home to work at 6:30 am. It was very difficult for me and my family going thru this routine. I had to completely disconnect myself from life and friends, but I knew that hard work will pay off for me in the end.

CPA exam was by far the most challenging commitment I put myself into . . . but it is not impossible to pass. It requires family support, dedication, and prioritizing studying; give and do your best and believe in yourself.

Now that I got my results a few days back and know I am done! It is time for me to compensate my family for being so busy the last five months.

—Rania Kabbara

As extreme as it may seem, Rania did get six to seven hours of sleep every day. Do not cut down the sleep to the extent that your health is affected. With a sickly body, you cannot concentrate and analyze effectively—two critical skills you need to pass the exam. In fact, you may want to sleep more in the last week of preparation to maintain a healthy mind and body.

Cut Down the Fun   In the cram mode you should not spend time doing anything that is considered fun. Tell yourself that you can wait until after the exam.

Put the 25-Hour-Day Suggestions to Extreme   Have you been outsourcing? Ask your outside help to work longer hours. Combining family time and study time? You might need to ask your family to sacrifice more so you can focus on your study in the last month.

This Will Not Be Easy, But Doable   The cram mode is not a desirable study tactic. It should only be implemented if you run out of time but want to beat the beast once and for all.

Exam-Taking Strategies

We went through the tips on how to best prepare for the exam. Here is another set of tips that you can use on the exam day.

Time Each Testlet

Time management is especially important for FAR and REG because many candidates struggle to complete these two sections. Although the pressure is generally less for AUD and BEC, you should still set a time limit for each testlet.

FAR   I generally recommend that you allocate no more than 45 minutes for each multiple-choice (MC) testlet and 90 minutes for the task-based simulation (TBS) testlet. There are three MC testlets and one TBS testlet, so this will take you 45 minutes × 3 + 90 minutes = 3 hours and 45 minutes, with 15 minutes as your buffer.

This means 1.5 minutes for each of the 90 MC questions and 13 minutes for each of the seven TBS questions.

It is important to stick with the discipline in your first MC testlet, because if you do well, you will be faced with two difficult testlets, which will take more time to finish. If you lag in the first one, you will most likely run out of the time in the TBS.

AUD   The duration and number of questions is the same as FAR, and therefore you can also allocate 1.5 minutes for each MC and 13 minutes for each TBS question.

You will likely finish before your own time limit. In this case you will have the luxury to spend more time on the TBS and score more points.

REG   Many candidates can barely finish REG. This means that having a strict discipline in time management is critical for REG.

There are three testlets with 24 MC questions instead of the 30 each in FAR and AUD. At the same time, you have only three hours instead of four. You can allocate 35 minutes instead for each multiple-choice testlet, 60 minutes for the TBS questions, and 15 minutes as the buffer. This means slightly less than 1.5 minutes for each MC question and 10 minutes for each of the six TBS questions.

BEC   Most candidates have more than enough time to finish BEC. As long as you target 45 minutes for each testlet (~1.5 minutes for each question) and an hour for the Written Communication tasks, you will have 15 minutes to spare. If English is not your first language, you might want to work faster on the MC question to have spare time for the business writing.

Testlets May Become More Difficult

We talked about the adaptive nature of the questions in Chapter 2, "What Is the CPA Exam?" and how you will get a more difficult testlet if you do well on the first set. The reality is that many candidates cannot gauge when a testlet has gotten harder, especially if you have prepared very well.

The best thing you can do is not to worry about the difficulty level. Focus on getting the questions right and move on.

Read the Questions and Answers Very Carefully

We discussed in Chapter 6 how some of the questions can be quite tricky. This is especially the case for AUD, because one word change can alter the meaning of the entire question. The "vagueness" of the question is also a killer for many candidates.

The answers can also be tricky. Unlike computational questions, the conceptual ones are more subjective and therefore all answers look more or less the same. There could even be more than one correct answer and you have to pick the best one.

One helpful way to differentiate the answer is to look for absolute negatives. For example, answers that use "all" or "never" could be offering a clue that the answer might be wrong, because in many cases things cannot be completely "all" in real life.

Make the Best Educated Guess

Certain test areas, such as Information Technology in BEC, are such vast topics that no CPA review course can cover all materials in detail. Do not let it haunt you if you come across something you have never seen in your life (maybe it is a pretest question, who knows). Just try your best—think logically and put yourself in the shoes of the examiners and determine what they are trying to test. Then, take a deep breath and move on.

Answer All Questions

The test is positively graded. Never leave an answer blank.

Do Not Second-Guess

Research has shown that when we are confronted with multiple-choice questions, our subconscious usually leads to the correct answer. Therefore, when you check your work and find that one previous question you did was wrong, triple-check before you change the answer. More likely than not, the original answer is correct.

Take the Break Wisely

For FAR and REG, do not think of wasting time doing anything but answering questions. For me, adrenaline is enough to keep me going.

But if you usually need one of those toilet breaks, test your limit before the exam. Set aside three to four hours so you can work on a mock exam. It is a good way to see what you can handle without the break.

Also, how you went through quickly or slowly in one section is not a good indicator of your performance in other sections. The best way to find out is to work on at least one mock exam for each section.

CHAPTER

How to Overcome the Fear of Task-Based Simulations

Task-based simulations are condensed case studies that test accounting knowledge and skills using real life work-related situations.

—CPA Exam Candidate Bulletin

In Financial Accounting and Reporting (FAR), Audit and Attestation (AUD), and Regulation (REG), the questions are presented in two formats: multiple-choice questions and task-based simulations, or TBS.

TBS is created to replace the long questions that existed in the pen-and-paper exam format prior to 2005. For each TBS, candidates have access to the authoritative literature, a calculator, spreadsheets, and other resources and tools, which they can use to demonstrate proficiency in applying the body of knowledge. There are seven TBS in FAR and AUD, and six TBS in REG. There are no TBS in Business Environment and Concepts (BEC).

TBS can never be "learned" because they can appear in many formats. Candidates should, however, try their best to get prepared because TBS represent 40 percent of the total score for FAR, AUD, and REG.

Study Tips

TBS can appear in any format in the actual exam. Instead of memorizing the simulation questions in your test prep software, you should focus on the following:

- Get familiar with the buttons and tools on the computer screen.
- Practice using the search function to look up the authoritative literature.
- Learn how to think on your feet and apply the relevant concepts.

Practice in a Simulated Testing Environment

At the very least, get familiar with the layout of the testing environment, including the buttons, search functions, and the calculator, as well as the best way to navigate between tasks. Do not spend time in the actual exam figuring them out.

The *Wiley Test Bank* is designed to closely simulate the real testing environment. You should take the time to attempt the 164 simulation questions contained in the complete set.

Do Not Wait until the Last Minute

I recommend that you set aside a few hours each week to go over the TBS after reviewing each topic. It is best to work on them right after you complete the multiple-choice questions in the same topic and have thoroughly gone through the explanation of each question. Because the nature of the questions can be quite different, you may need to work on quite a number of TBS before you can try out all the features.

TBS is a good way to help you nail down the concepts because it forces you to think about a question in different perspectives. It is beneficial for you to treat this as an integrated part of your own study program.

Make Use of the Free Access

The search function used in the CPA exam is similar but different from the typical search engines we use for online research.

To facilitate practicing this specific skill before the exam, the American Institute of Certified Public Accountants (AICPA) grants each eligible exam candidate a six-month free subscription to its Authoritative Literature, an online access to professional literature used in the CPA exam. Make good use of this tool.

Highlight Keywords in Each Important Topic

Ideally it would be a great help if you remember the Internal Revenue Code for REG and the Auditing Standard Code for AUD.

For those who cannot afford the time and effort for this extra work, get familiar with the keywords in the heavily tested area. This increases your speed and accuracy when you use the research function and you will be able to tackle the simulations more efficiently.

How You Study the MC Questions May Affect Your Performance in Simulations

A reader has shared with me this great tip in preparing for TBS. When she prepared for her first exam, she practiced on the MC questions and marked them off from the answer without looking closely at the explanation. This was especially the case if she got the answer correct the first time. In the actual exam, she thought she did fine on the simulations but ended up bombing that part based on the diagnostic report.

In preparation for her second exam, she changed her study tactics. For all the MC questions, whether she got it right or wrong, she took a good look and understood the reason why. It took much more time to go through each question this way, but because she knew the concept she could afford more time on the practice problems. It was a far superior tactic for her because after this "training," when she looked at any simulation question, a relevant concept would pop up in her mind.

When she took the exam she was much more confident of passing when walking out of the testing center. And she did pass with an 86.

Exam-Taking Strategies

Besides knowing how to study for the exam, knowing how to perform on the exam day is equally important.

Read the Questions Carefully

TBS can be overwhelming because it can appear in all shapes and sizes. You have to read the question very carefully and make sure you understand what is being asked.

Fill in Everything

You find this advice throughout the book. The CPA exam does not penalize for wrong answers, so it is better to blind guess than to leave anything blank.

If you run out of time, go straight to questions with drop-down menus (rather than those that require a typed in answer) because you have a much higher chance of getting them right.

> Dear Stephanie, I wrote FAR on the 30th last month. The multiple choice questions were ok but the simulations were very lengthy. I ran out of time. I tried to put at least something in the answer choices. I don't know what will happen. Just wanted to share with you. As soon as I get my result I will let you know.
>
> **—Shilpi**

You may want to know that Shilpi did pass the FAR section of the exam.

Time Management

We went over this in the previous chapter. Here is the summary.

For FAR and AUD, allocate 90 minutes for TBS. Because there are seven questions, spend 13 minutes or less on each question. For REG, allocate 60 minutes for TBS. There are six questions, so spend 10 minutes or less on each question. This matches with the suggestion from the *CPA Exam Candidate Bulletin*, in which candidates are expected to spend 8 to 15 minutes on each simulation question.

Do You Have Other Suggestions?

I received quite a few insightful comments from readers on the topic of simulations. Here is one from Lori, who passed all four sections on her first attempt. If you have other thoughts on how to tackle this and other parts of the exam, please share with me—I would love to feature your ideas in the next edition of my book.

> Hi Stephanie, you told me that simulations can never be learned. I think you are right and wrong. It's true that sims can appear in any format and it is hard to teach people how to do well on sims except to tell them "go study the concepts."
>
> I would say that candidates like me can "learn" how to do well on simulations by understanding all the "what if" scenarios. When we study a topic, don't focus on what the CPA review book tells us. We should put the topic in the context of a scenario and think about how it can be applied in our everyday lives. In my opinion, this is why the examiners come up with the idea of simulations anyway, to tell us that you can't rely on spoon feeding from the review courses to pass this exam.
>
> By the way, I passed BEC, my last part. Thanks for all your help!
>
> **—Lori**

How to Ace the Written Communication Tasks

For each of three written communication tasks, candidates must read a scenario and then write an appropriate document relating to the scenario. The instructions state what form the document should take (such as a memo or letter) and its focus. The candidate's response should provide the correct information in writing that is clear, complete, and professional.

—CPA Exam Candidate Bulletin

The Written Communication task is part of the Business Environment and Concepts (BEC) exam representing 15 percent of the total score. Unless you aim for a perfect score in the multiple-choice questions, how you gain points in these three pieces of writing can make or break your passing success. For international candidates whose English is not their first language, this poses additional challenges.

Now, let us look at what the CPA exam graders are looking for, and how you can score points accordingly.

What Are the Examiners Looking For?

The examiners want to test the candidates' ability to produce business writing that is commonly performed by a junior accountant. To earn points for this section, candidates should demonstrate:

- Understanding and accurate interpretation of the task
- Writing a document that relates or responds to the objective
- Writing in a clear and professional manner

In other words, the examiners look for:

- Complete sentences
- Use of standard English
- Relevance
- Clarity
- Conciseness
- Good organization
- Proper formatting with introduction and conclusion

I explain how you can achieve that with the following tips.

Seven Tips for Writing Success

Complete Sentences: Avoid Bullet Points and Charts

In the old days, CPA exam candidates were asked to write as long as possible, stuffing each paragraph with all the concepts they could think of in order to score maximum points, and writing in bullet points made keywords stand out.

The rule has changed.

The reason is actually more technical than anything else—your answers will be graded by not only humans, but also machines. Machines are programmed to check grammar and sentence structures. Bullet points and number lists are mostly not complete sentences and you will lose points. Machines cannot read charts, diagrams, and graphics and therefore these should be avoided.

Use of Standard English: Stick to Standard Business Writing Format

If you have some working experience from an internship or a full-time job, you will understand what is meant by professional business writing. Drafting a business memo or a letter to a client should be fairly easy for you, but you might want to pay special attention to the following.

Use Standard Grammar, Punctuation, Spelling, and Word Usage   If the keyword is a technical term or an abbreviation, spell it out in full with the abbreviation in parenthesis. For example, "ERP" should be spelled out fully as "Enterprise Resource Planning (ERP)." Once the term is defined, it is fine to use the acronym throughout the rest of the writing.

Exclude nonstandard punctuations and excessive exclamation marks, which is inappropriate in business writing. Casual expressions such as "I'd," "we'll," "let's" and abbreviated wordings used in text messages should also be avoided.

If a mathematical formula is involved when defining an accounting concept, describe the formula in standard English instead of using mathematical signs in the writing.

Note

From now until you pass the CPA exam, stop using the abbreviations commonly used in text messaging. Practice using properly spelled English words in all aspects of everyday life, including communications on social media and email to friends. You want to have the correct words flowing naturally on the exam day.

Use American English I am not sure whether the electronic scoring system gives credit to British spelling of certain words, but given that this is a U.S. exam, I recommend that you stick with American English whenever possible. Here are the common spelling differences between American and British English:

- *-or* versus *-our* (e.g., color, humor versus colour, humour).
- *-er* versus *-re* (e.g., center, meter versus centre, metre).
- *-se* versus *-ce* (e.g., license versus licence).
- *-ze* versus *-se* (e.g., organize, recognize, analyze versus organise, recognise, analyse).
- *-og* versus *-ogue* (e.g., catalog versus catalogue).
- *-m* versus *-mme* (e.g., program versus programme).

The best way to ensure correct spelling is to use the spell-check function. It is also a valuable tool to minimize careless mistakes.

Relevance: Aim to Stay "On Topic" versus Being "Correct"

The three pieces of written communications are *not* graded based on the technical accuracy of the content, but on whether the content is relevant. In other words, you simply need to stay on topic. This can be easily done by using topic keywords in your essay.

Clarity: Include Elaboration and Summary

As long as you can demonstrate knowledge of the subject by providing details with examples, definitions, and other ways to develop your ideas, that's a good enough job to pass this part of the exam.

Conciseness: Less Is More

Avoid writing more than what is needed. Do not repeat the same idea in different paragraphs.

Good Organization: Structure Your Answer Before Writing

Write down your basic ideas on the note card and make sure that your document has a clear introduction, main body, and conclusion. Start with an overview where you describe the purpose or intent of the document, which you can do by rewriting (but not copying) the question. Then, ensure that your following paragraphs support this overview, and lead into each other well. Complete the task with one simple, standard conclusion common in business writing.

Manage Your Time

Be conscious of your time limit. It is important that you have enough time to complete the introduction, the middle paragraphs, and a conclusion.

Seven Steps to Creating a Great Piece of Business Writing

Now that you know what the examiners are looking for, let us go over the steps on how to ace this part of the exam.

Step 1. Identify the Format, Objective, Your Role, and Your Audience

The question typically starts with the description of a scenario and a particular issue that you need to solve or a task that you need to perform. The first step is for you to identify the following.

What You Are Being Asked to Do (Format and Objective)   The format is most likely a business memo, a letter, or an email. The objective, or question requirement, is often explicitly written in the question.

Who You Are (Role)   Although in many cases you take the role of a junior accountant to prepare a business document for your supervisor, you may be asked to be an assistant manager explaining an accounting concept to first-year accountants; or you could be the engagement manager addressing a complaint from a client.

The tone of your business writing should be adjusted based on your role as a supervisor, peer, subordinate, advisor, or independent auditor.

To Whom You Address the Business Writing (Audience)   Your audience varies in a greater degree—from entry-level accountants, supervisor, to clients and regulatory bodies. The tone of your writing should be adjusted based on seniority as well as the perceived technical knowledge of the audience.

Step 2. Identify Keywords Related to the Objective

On the note card, write down the core keywords in the question. From each keyword, brainstorm related keywords such as concepts, technical terms, and application of the concepts.

Step 3. Write Down the First Sentence of Each Paragraph

Think carefully about the flow of the writing and construct the first sentence of each paragraph to set up the framework.

The first sentence in each paragraph should always contain the main idea; the follow-on sentences (which you will work on in Step 5) are used to expand the idea with further explanation and examples.

All paragraphs are to be grouped into:

- **First paragraph**: An introduction where you address the audience and summarize the objective as stated in the question.
- **Main body** (one to two paragraphs): The first paragraph within the main body should present the core concepts or your main position. Additional paragraphs can be added as you develop your ideas to support your core concept/position.
- **Last paragraph**: A conclusion written in a simple but professional manner.

Step 4. Begin the First Sentence by Rewriting the Question

For example, if you are asked to explain the difference between capital lease and operating lease to a client, then you can begin by writing

"The purpose of this memo is to define capital lease and operating lease and explain the concepts behind the two different accounting treatments." The keywords used in this case are "capital lease," "operating lease," and "different." I think "accounting treatment" can score some points as well.

What You Should Do

- Identify the keywords used in the question.
- Rewrite the question using the keywords.
- Most of the time, you can start the paragraph by stating "the purpose of this memo/letter is to" followed by the rewriting of the question.

Step 5. State the Core Concept/Position and Develop Ideas in Separate Paragraphs

The first paragraph within the main body is typically used to define the core keywords based on relevant accounting concepts. Then, develop your ideas based on this concept and expand each idea in separate paragraphs. Try your best to use the secondary set of related keywords that you brainstormed on the note card.

These ideas may include:

- Related accounting concepts
- Common application
- Benefits and limitations of the accounting treatment
- Impact to the client company

What You Should Do

- Write with business sense. You can express your opinion and include examples to support your ideas.
- Compose in a tone that is appropriate to the audience.
- Use spell-check function.

What You Should Not Do

- Include bullets and number lists.
- Use undefined abbreviations.

Step 6. Keep the Conclusion Simple and Professional

The following ending paragraphs are among the most common in American business writing:

- I would be happy to discuss these issues with you at your earliest convenience.
- Feel free to contact me if you have further questions on this topic.
- I look forward to working with you to further discuss the situation in detail.

In other parts of the world, phrases such as "I would be most obliged" are commonly used but may be considered too formal in the United States.

Step 7. Proofread from Beginning to End

It is important to click on the spell-check button to identify obvious typos and mistakes. Also spend the time to:

- Reread the question: Did you interpret the question correctly?
- Proofread the entire piece to check the flow, content, word choice, and sentence structure.

A Note on Reference Books

The American Institute of Certified Public Accountants (AICPA) recommends three reference books for the preparation of the Written Communications task. Among the three, my choice is *The Elements of Style* by Strunk and White. I read this little book in college when I took a popular academic and professional writing course (nicknamed the Little Red Schoolhouse) at the University of Chicago. It is a delightful read full of practical examples.

The Written Communication tasks can be tricky but is definitely doable. In fact, it can be straightforward if we follow these seven steps. Good luck!

Note

I have a more detailed book review on *The Elements of Style* on my site: http://ipassthecpaexam.com/elements-of-style-review.

You may also want to check out this collection of grammar and writing resources compiled by the University of Chicago: http://writing-program.uchicago.edu/resources/grammar.htm.

10

Audit and Attestation (AUD)

T he CPA, after all, is a qualification for Certified *Public* Accountant. It should not come as a surprise that examiners are looking for advanced (and working) knowledge of a public accountant's classic job—audit and attestation (AUD).

What Does AUD Cover?

Here is the examination specification released by the American Institute of Certified Public Accountants (AICPA):

- Engagement acceptance and understanding the assignment (12 to 16 percent).
- Understanding the entity and its environment (16 to 20 percent).
- Performing audit procedures and evaluating evidence (16 to 20 percent).
- Evaluating audit findings, communications, and reporting (16 to 20 percent).
- Accounting and review services engagements (12 to 16 percent).
- Professional responsibilities (16 to 20 percent).

This is a four-hour examination, with three testlets each containing 30 multiple-choice questions, and one testlet containing seven task-based simulation (TBS) questions. Multiple-choice represents 50 to 60 percent of the score with TBS representing the rest. The multiple-choice questions are adaptive but the TBSs are not.

Pass Rate History and Trend

The CPA exam pass rate for the AUD section is more or less the same as the rest: It hovers around 50 percent in recent years (Figure 10.1). Although the CPA exam pass rate has been steadily increasing over the years, it seems to have gone down since the next exam format was introduced in 2011.

Number One Concern about AUD

Many readers worry about AUD because they have never done an audit. The good news is that auditing is all about examining and analyzing procedures and finance statements in a systematic manner. It is a detailed process and there is a lot of memorization involved, but the concepts are not difficult.

Having said that, direct or indirect work experience related to auditing does help a lot when it comes to AUD.

Let's take me as an example. I have never been an auditor and I am not an accounting major, but my work in the corporate finance department of a publicly listed company and my everyday interaction with the auditors is the number one reason why I passed the AUD exam relatively easily on my first attempt.

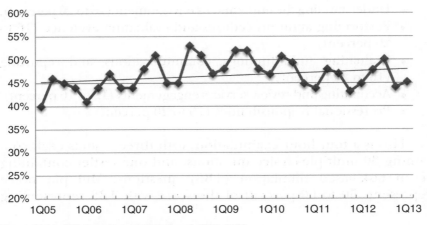

Figure 10.1   AUD Exam Passing Rate Trend, 2005–2012

Source: www.aicpa.org.

How You Study Depends Largely on Your Background   If you are an auditor, you have distinct advantages no matter how junior you may be. The examination covers exactly what you do on a daily basis, and you understand what the examiners are looking for.

If you work in an accounting department in a corporation, you have an advantage because you are familiar with the audit procedure from a client's perspective.

If you are just out of college with an accounting degree, you are fine because you are fresh with the theories, but you should put in the effort to understand the audit procedure (in the real world) to compensate for the lack of working knowledge.

If you do not fall into the above categories, you need to work harder because most candidates will have an edge over you. The examiners expect all candidates to have a good understanding of the audit from start to finish and you will be surprised at the level of detail in the multiple-choice questions.

Anyway, don't let me scare you—I am confident that you can pass if you follow these study tips.

Study Tips

Here are some suggestions on how you can prepare for the exam effectively and efficiently.

Take AUD Immediately after FAR

If you understand accounting, you will agree with me that FAR (financial accounting) and AUD (auditing the financial accounts of companies) are interrelated. Therefore, it is not surprising that you will see many references to FAR in the AUD exam. This is the case for both multiple-choice and simulation testlets. That is why I recommend AUD to be your second section, immediately after FAR.

After all, an auditor's main job is to verify with reasonable assurance that FAR has been applied in accordance with generally accepted accounting principles (GAAP).

Switch Your Brain to Memorization Mode

Although working knowledge is helpful, AUD is an academic exam and studying relies heavily on memorization. At the same time, it is equally important that you know how to apply the concepts in an actual business environment.

Note

I also suggest that you study the financial ratios in FAR. Auditors rely heavily on financial ratios to look for unusual trends in analytical procedure. It should not come as a surprise if financial ratios are used as part of the questions in AUD.

Memorize the "Important" Sample Reports   I know some people think it is not necessary to memorize the whole report, but everyone agrees that you have to remember the important points in the audit report, for example, which specific sentence should appear in which audit opinion, and where in the paragraphs—yes, it gets that specific.

The audit opinion is like a "cheat sheet" for your entire AUD exam. The conclusion of the audit objective and findings is summarized in the audit opinion. Every sentence in the audit opinion is there for a reason, and the examiners will ask you all these reasons in the exam.

How to Memorize the Audit Report   The focus should be on the unqualified audit report. My method was to separate the audit report into several sections—and it is quite clear why the wordings have to be there if you put in the effort to understand the reasons behind the audit report.

Then, hand copy the entire report a few times—reading it aloud as you copy will help. The good news is that it is not rocket science; all it asks for is patience and practice.

For the other qualified audit reports, compilations, and reviews, I do not think you need to memorize them but you have to know the differences between them.

Use Flash Cards   Because AUD is more a conceptual exam, flash cards are excellent study tools especially for writing down the AUD mnemonics and concepts. We discussed how you can prepare your own flash cards or make the best use of purchased flash cards in Chapter 7, "Study Tips and Exam-Taking Strategies."

Get Familiar with Internal Control   Since Enron, Worldcom, Lehman Brothers, and other big corporate failures, there has been a big emphasis on internal control everywhere, including the CPA exam. You may notice that internal control represents only 16 to 20 percent of the AUD section, but similar concepts pop up (e.g., how weak internal control will affect the conclusion of your audit findings) throughout the exam so it is an important concept to know by heart.

My strategy is to work on many practice questions on this topic so you are well covered in all scenarios within internal control. Most importantly, redo the wrong ones (twice at least) so the right concepts sink in.

Visualize What Auditors Do in Real Life   This is not mainstream advice; in fact, I have never seen it suggested anywhere, but I consider this an important "secret" to help you pass the exam.

Some people think AUD is easy while others insist it is impossible. I think the difference is whether you can really understand what an auditor does. My suggestion is for you to find an auditor (a friend, a college alum . . . or contact the CPA Society of your state for help) and ask them to walk you through what they do in terms of the audit process. I can almost guarantee you that things start to click once you know what they do, how they do it, and why.

Exam-Taking Strategies

Studying is usually relatively easy for AUD because the topics tend to build on one another. Having said that, most questions are conceptual in nature and they can be tricky.

It is important that you work on the practice questions and get used to the format of the questions. In particular, if you see a "pattern of error," for example, that you are always misreading certain types of questions, or picking the first answer that seems to be correct versus the best answer, then you must learn to answer these questions correctly. You can refer to the exam-taking tips discussed in Chapter 7.

Presenting the Outline

Below is the outline of the AUD exam content as well as suggestions on how to approach the review materials. The outline is written based on the *Wiley CPA Exam Review* but the tips are applicable to other review courses.

Module 1: Professional Responsibilities

This section represents 16 to 20 percent of the tested content. You can see the majority of questions coming from the AICPA Code of Professional Conduct.

The names and acronyms of the professional bodies are similar and could be confusing especially to international candidates. This is a straightforward section once you take the time to recognize the names.

AICPA Code of Professional Conduct

This section provides an overview of the AICPA Code of Professional Conduct and the outline of the conduct code. Although you do not need to memorize the outline, I strongly encourage you to read through the pages to get a macro understanding of a CPA's responsibilities. The concepts covered in the AUD study module are based on these principles.

I also suggest a quick review of the Code one day before the exam. Candidates are often asked to find particular information from the Code using the research function in simulation questions. Having a basic idea of the keywords contained in the Code can help immensely in the research.

The Sarbanes-Oxley Act of 2002

The Sarbanes-Oxley Act is an important topic covered in AUD, Business Environment and Concept (BEC), and Regulation (REG). In this section you find the relevant sections of the Act (Titles I–IV).

Public Company Accounting Oversight Board (PCAOB)

The Sarbanes-Oxley Act authorizes the establishment of PCAOB. This section primarily focuses on the authority and roles of the Board.

International Standards—Ethical

The International Ethics Standards Board for Accountants (IESBA) is a body within the International Federation of Accountants (IFAC), of which the AICPA is a member.

The IESBA issues ethical standards for accountants around the world. You can see this as the international version of the AICPA Code of Professional Conduct.

International Standards—Auditing/Assurance

The international auditing standards are developed by the International Auditing and Assurance Standards Board (IAASB) of the IFAC.

The international auditing standards aim to develop a consistent professional standard and are not meant to override the auditing standards of its members.

It is important to understand the major difference between IAASB standards and U.S. generally accepted auditing standards (GAAS). You can find a list and a table in the review materials for easy reference.

Other

There are a number of related professional and regulatory bodies that you should know for the purpose of the CPA exam:

- Securities and Exchange Commission (SEC)
- Government Accountability Office (GAO)
- Department of Labor (DOL)

Module 2: Engagement Planning and Assessing Risks

This module discusses the requirements relating to two standards of fieldwork: engagement planning and risk assessment.

Basic Concepts

This section goes through the following key concepts.

Financial Statement Assertions Management is responsible for the fair presentation of financial statements.

Audit Risk An audit must be designed to limit audit risk to an appropriately low level.

Materiality According to Statements on Auditing Standards (SAS) 107, materiality is "the magnitude of an omission or misstatement of accounting information that, in the light of surrounding circumstances, make it probable that the judgment of a reasonable person relying on the information would have been changed or influenced by the omission or misstatement."

Errors and Fraud Understand the difference between error and fraud (fraud is error done intentionally). Auditors aim to obtain reasonable assurance on whether the financial statements are free of material errors and fraud. Note the key terms *reasonable assurance* and *material*—auditors do not and cannot guarantee that the financial statements are totally free of errors and fraud.

Illegal Acts This is a heavily tested topic. Candidates should focus on whether the illegal acts have direct or indirect impacts on the financial statements. The responsibility of the auditor is different in each case.

Audit Planning

Audit planning is the first step of the audit procedure. Candidates should be familiar with the details of each of these steps:

- Communicating with predecessor auditors.
- Establishing an understanding with the client (engagement letters).
- Evaluating whether it is appropriate to take on the engagement.
- Developing an overall strategy (scope, objective, focus).
- Developing and documenting an audit plan.
- Preparing a written audit program.
- Performing tests of control and substantive tests.

Obtain an Understanding of the Entity and Its Environment

Auditors perform risk assessment procedures to obtain the understanding of the entity. This can be done by:

- Communication with predecessor auditors
- Analytical procedure

- Consideration of internal control
- Supervision requirements

Assess the Risks of Material Misstatement and Design Further Audit Procedures

This is part of the risk assessment procedure. The auditor is required to identify significant risks that require the focus of the audit team.

One-off and complex transactions are more likely to give rise to significant risks. Candidates are expected to know how these risks can be identified.

Quality Control

The Statements on Quality Control Standards (SQCS) are quality control standards applied to the CPA firm. CPA firms undergo a peer review performed by a CPA or a CPA firm. You should understand the two types of peer review, their respective procedures, and the differences between them.

Module 3: Understanding Internal Control and Assessing Control Risk

Internal control is an important topic in the CPA exam. You can expect to see numerous questions on how a specific control procedure can detect a weakness or error, and its relationship/interaction with the other procedures in the audit.

It is important to understand that internal control is part of each stage; it is especially important to obtain understanding and risk assessment and to perform further audit procedures.

The Nature of Internal Control

Internal control is a key concept tested primarily in AUD but also in BEC (under IT) and REG (professional responsibilities). This section discusses the definition of international control and the five major components.

The Auditor's Consideration of Internal Control

This section primarily focuses on how the concept of internal control is applied to various stages in the audit procedure.

In particular, candidates should understand the auditor's role in the following:

- Obtaining and documenting understanding of internal control.
- Assessing risk of material misstatement and designing further audit procedure.
- Performing tests of controls and evaluating results.

The concept is not difficult but the questions can be tricky. You may be asked how a specific control procedure can detect a weakness or error in multiple-choice questions. There could be more than one correct answer and you have to select the best answer.

The most effective way to learn how internal control can be applied in different aspects of the audit is to work on as many practice questions as possible, including the ones from task-based simulations.

Audits (Examinations) of Internal Control

An integrated audit of SEC registrants (public companies) that provide assurance about the fairness of financial statements and the effectiveness of internal control is required under the Sarbanes-Oxley Act of 2002. This means that auditors are now focusing more on internal control than on substantive procedures.

The PCAOB Standard has the following structure:

Plan the Audit   The planning phase is similar to that in the audit of the financial statement. The focus is on who the auditor can address about the risk of fraud and management override.

Use a Top-Down Approach to Identify Controls to Test   A top-down approach starts at the financial statement level, followed by identifying significant accounts and disclosures, then by relevant assertions. To obtain further understanding of likely sources of misstatement, auditors should also understand the flow of the transactions and identify controls implemented by management to address potential misstatements and detect unauthorized use of assets.

Test Design and Operating Effectiveness of Controls   When testing the design and operating effectiveness of internal control, the auditor needs to express an overall opinion on internal control instead of the opinion on each part of individual control.

Evaluate Identified Deficiencies   The severity of a deficiency depends on the possibility of that control failing to prevent or detect a misstatement, and the magnitude of this potential misstatement.

Wrap-Up   The auditor should form an opinion and obtain written representation from the client. The auditor should also communicate (in writing) the following important matters with the management and audit committee prior to issuing the report on internal control:

- Material weakness.
- Significant deficiencies.
- Significant deficiencies that are not corrected but are previously communicated.

Report on Internal Control   This section discusses the major points in the report. It is best to study these points by referring to the sample unqualified audit report on internal control. In my opinion, copying the entire report a few times is one of the best ways to memorize these important points in the report.

There is also a discussion on the difference between PCAOB Standard 5 and Statements on Standards for Attestation Engagements (SSAE) 15, as well as PCAOB Standard 4 related to reporting on previously reported material weakness.

Accounting Cycles

It is important to understand the accounting cycle in order to answer questions in the AUD exam. For example, candidates may be asked to identify an audit test or internal control strengths and weaknesses in a particular stage of a transaction cycle.

Go through the details in each of the following accounting cycles in the review materials:

- Sales, receivables, and cash receipts
- Purchases, payables, and cash disbursements
- Inventories and production
- Personnel and payroll

- Financing
- Investing

Note

It may be helpful to revise the flow chart symbols in case the questions use flow charts to present the accounting cycles. A more detailed discussion can be found in Chapter 13, "Business Environment and Concepts (BEC)," under Module 41 on Information Technology.

Other Considerations

Additional Financial Statement Audit Communications   Auditors should communicate significant deficiencies and material weakness to the management and those charged with governance (i.e., the board of directors and audit committee). Remember the role of the audit committee.

Effects of an Internal Audit Function   In this section you need to know how internal audit work affects the external audit: the work of an internal audit may affect the nature, timing, and extent of the audit procedure, and internal auditors may provide direct assistance in performing some of the procedures. Competence and objectivity are two important attributes of internal auditors.

Module 4: Responding to Risk Assessment

We went over the test of controls in Module 3. This module focuses on another audit procedure—the substantive tests. Expect many questions on audit evidence in the CPA exam.

Evidence—General

Audit evidence is the gathering of information used by the auditor to arrive at the conclusion to be issued in the report. Note that the concepts of "existence" and "completeness" are important here. You should also understand the meaning of "sufficient" and "appropriate" evidence, as well as the types of audit evidence.

Evidence—Specific (Substantive Procedures)

This section covers the substantive procedures, which are used to directly test the financial statement. The major types of substantive procedures include substantive analytical procedure and tests of details of transactions, account balances, and disclosures. You will find a useful summary of audit procedures in the review materials for each item in the financial statement.

Other Specific Audit Evidence Topics

This section goes through in relative detail how each of the following financial statement items can be examined.

Review of compliance disclosure, management inquiry, and review of agreements are commonly done in most cases, but there are special auditing procedures that apply to particular financial statement items. For example, confirmation should be done for receivables and observation of stock counts should be done in the case of inventory.

- Cash
- Receivables
- Inventory
- Investment Securities
- Property, plant, and equipment
- Prepaid assets
- Payables
- Long-term debt
- Owners' equity
- Revenue
- Expenses
- Client representation letters
- Using the work of a specialist
- Loss contingencies and inquiry of a client's lawyer
- Fair value
- Related-party transactions
- Subsequent events
- Omitted procedures discovered after the report date
- Statement of cash flows

If you have done an audit before, you will find this an easy section to handle, but you do need to remember the steps and details of the procedures. For those who have never done an audit before, analytic procedure is simply a systematic way to analyze the financial statements. The methods are different for each item but the concept is similar. You can spend more time on the practice questions to get a better idea how this can be done.

Completing the Audit

This section discusses the steps to complete the audit, including the necessary audit procedures, examining whether the material misstatement identified has been corrected, and engagement quality review.

Note

The amount of study required for this module largely depends on how well you understand the work of an audit. If this is your everyday job, I recommend that you only skim through (or even skip) the review materials and go straight to the practice questions. If auditing is new to you, then you do need to spend the time reviewing each of the audit procedures and understand how they should be applied, followed by lots of practice using the test preparation software.

Module 5: Reporting

This module focuses on the various reports prepared by the auditors. The goal is to study very hard the details of the unqualified audit report, and study the other reports enough such that you can tell the difference between them.

Financial Statement Audit Report—General

There are four primary forms of "Accountant Associations":

1. Examination: Provide a positive opinion with reasonable assurance.
2. Review: Provide limited assurance (i.e., negative assurance).
3. Agreed-upon procedures: Provide summary of findings.
4. Compilations: Provide no assurance.

Candidates should be aware of the restricted-use reports and general-use reports. Restricted-use reports are intended for specific purposes and typically for specific parties, for example, internal management and board of directors.

Take the time to study the audit report for nonpublic companies and public companies and identify the differences between them.

Financial Statement Audit Reports—Detailed

There are times when the unqualified report requires additional explanation, or when the auditors need to issue a qualified opinion instead. You should get familiar with how each special situation may affect the reporting. The most common examples are listed in the review materials and these are the ones that you must know for the purpose of this exam.

Accountant Association Other Than Audits

This section goes through the other reports that can be prepared by auditors, such as the unaudited statements, compiled or review statements, and reviewed interim statements. Candidates should note the difference between an audit report and these reports in terms of purpose and wording used.

Reporting on Compliance

As the name suggests, a compliance report relates to whether an organization has complied with the requirements of various laws and regulations. Compliance has become significantly more important in the past few years and you should expect to see quite a few questions on this topic. Compliance auditing is often used for governmental agencies and your basic knowledge in governmental accounting may be useful in this case.

Module 6: Accounting and Review Services

This module discusses two common types of engagements performed by accountants other than the audit—compilation and review. The professional standards on compilations and reviews are much shorter, but the fact that you need to apply the correct standards can be difficult.

Financial Statement Compilations

Nature of Compilations   The engagement involves assisting the management to present the financial information in the form of a financial statement. The major difference between compilation and audit is that the former provides no assurance.

Planning Compilations   The accountants generally make inquiries to get a better understanding of the business and the management. This understanding should be documented and communicated with management.

Compilation Procedures   The accountants should read the compiled statement for appropriate format and obvious material misstatement based on the understanding of the client's business. The accountants do not need to make further inquiry and perform any test of controls and analytical procedures.

Overall Compilation Reporting Issues   Special circumstances are discussed in this section, such as the resolution if the financial statement departs from GAAP or there is an inconsistent use of GAAP.

Financial Statement Reviews

Nature of Reviews   The objective of a review is somewhere in the middle between an audit and compilation—the purpose is to obtain a limited assurance, also known as *negative assurance* (i.e., no material modification is required). The accountant should gather review evidence to obtain a limited level of assurance for this engagement.

Planning Reviews   Similar to compilations, the accountants make inquiries to get a better understanding of the business and the management. Unlike compilations, an engagement letter must be prepared to specify the objective of the review engagement, the responsibilities of all parties (management and accountant), and the limitation of the engagement.

Review Procedures   The objective is to obtain limited assurance that no material modifications are needed. The amount of work is more substantial than a compilation but less substantial than an audit.

In particular, a review does not require the accountants to:

- Obtain an understanding of the internal control.
- Assess fraud risk.
- Test accounting records.
- Examine source documents.

Note that a representation letter signed by the management is required.

Overall Review Reporting Issues   Similar to the section under compilation, special circumstances are discussed in this section, such as the resolution if the financial statement departs from GAAP or there is an inconsistent use of GAAP.

Module 7: Audit Sampling

Audit sampling is an important technique used in tests of controls and substantive tests.

Basic Audit Sampling Concepts

Audit sampling is performed because it is either impossible or too costly to perform audit procedures on every item. Audit sampling can be divided into statistical and nonstatistical, and statistical sampling is used to help auditors design an efficient sample and evaluate sample results. For the purpose of this exam, you should know the two types of statistical sampling: attributes sampling and variable sampling.

You should understand the purpose of audit sampling and the concept of audit risk (audit risk = inherent risk × control risk × detection risk).

Sampling in Tests of Controls

This is a more in-depth discussion on sampling risk and detailed steps involved in attributes sampling. Candidates are expected to perform calculations based on these steps.

Sampling in Substantive Tests of Details

This section goes through a similar discussion on sampling risk applicable to substantive tests. The concept is similar but terminologies can be different.

Module 8: Auditing with Technology

This module focuses on the auditing procedure related to information technology. You can study this module together with Module 41, "Information Technology," in the BEC section of the exam.

An Auditor's Consideration of Internal Control When a Computer Is Present

The auditor's work on internal control is the same regardless of the existence of a computer system. However, the auditor may need to perform additional tests on application controls.

There is also an overview of the Computer-Assisted Audit Tools (CAAT) for tests of controls. Auditors carry out various techniques to:

- Understand the client's program.
- Test the program using auditor-controlled data.
- Introduce dummy transactions into a system.
- Capture audit data if the client's system does not retain permanent audit trials.
- Review the operating system and software.

Computer-Assisted Audit Tools

This is a brief overview of the various computerized audit tools. Examples include:

- Generalized Audit Software (GAS)
- Electronic spreadsheets
- Automated work paper software
- Database management system
- Text retrieval software
- Public databases
- Word processing software

Read through the review materials and learn about the functions of these tools. It is not necessary to memorize the details.

Reader's Sharing

What do my readers think about the AUD exam? Most find it relatively straightforward and there are fewer surprises than the other three sections. The simulation questions can show up in any format, and the best way to get prepared is to learn how to use the research tool effectively. A reader told me how the research tool worked like an open book for him because he was able to find answers for the other simulation questions.

You will do well if you prepare the right way. Good luck!

11

Financial Accounting and Reporting (FAR)

There is no question that the majority of CPA candidates find Financial Accounting and Reporting (FAR) the toughest section. It is probably not the most difficult, but the sheer volume of material overwhelms even the experienced accountants. Are you ready?

What Does FAR Cover?

Here is the examination specification released by the American Institute of Certified Public Accountants (AICPA):

- Conceptual framework, standards, standard setting, and presentation of financial statements (17 to 23 percent).
- Financial statement accounts: recognition, measurement, valuation, calculation, presentation, and disclosures (27 to 33 percent).
- Specific transactions, events, and disclosures: recognition, measurement, valuation, calculation, presentation, and disclosures (27 to 33 percent).
- Governmental accounting and reporting (8 to 12 percent).
- Not-for-profit (nongovernmental) accounting and reporting (8 to 12 percent).

Similar to AUD, this is a four-hour examination, with three testlets each containing 30 multiple-choice questions, and one testlet containing seven task-based simulation questions. The multiple-choice questions are adaptive but the simulation questions are not.

Passing Rate History and Trend

Although there has been marked improvement since 2005, the 2012 passing rate is still lower than 50 percent level at 48.0 percent (Figure 11.1). Within 2012, the passing rates fluctuate considerably from 43.8 percent to in the first quarter to 53.9 percent in the third quarter.

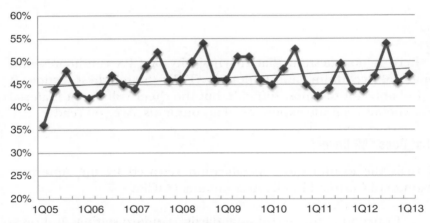

Figure 11.1   FAR Exam Passing Rate Trend, 2005–2012

Source: www.aicpa.org.

Study and Exam-Taking Tips

Here are some suggestions on how you can prepare for the exam effectively and efficiently.

I Recommend Tackling FAR First. Why?

In Chapters 2 and 5, I suggested taking FAR first when we talked about the sequence of exam taking. Here is a more extensive explanation.

FAR Preparation Eats Up a Lot of Time   No matter how you look at it, FAR takes a ton of preparation time. You will be glad to get rid of this biggest beast first.

The 18-Month Rule Consideration   This is the most important reason behind my recommendation. Since you only have 18 months to pass all four sections of the exam and the clock starts to tick once you pass the first one, it makes sense to complete the most time-consuming section first—in case you fail it a few times, your clock will still wait for you.

Double Benefit The good news is that FAR questions are mostly computational. The beauty of computational questions is that if you perform the calculations correctly, you will most likely get the correct answer. This is different from the other three sections (AUD in particular), in which the questions tend to be vague and there could be more than one correct answer. In short, if you allow sufficient study time to cover all the topics, you will likely pass. It will be a "double benefit" for completing the biggest section and earning a quick win.

Time Management Is Key to Success

We are talking about time management at two levels: during studying and during the exam.

When creating your study plan, you should schedule sufficient time for a comprehensive review. If you allow three months to study, aim to complete the review and practice questions within the first two months, and reserve the last month for catch up and final review. If you cannot complete the review in two months, it is better to extend the time to 2.5 or even 3 months (i.e., 3.5 to 4 months of preparation time including the buffer) to make it work.

During the exam, time your process so that you do not run out of time. Time is tight for many candidates in this section.

My Own Experience on FAR   I find bonds and leases really difficult even though I worked on several Yankee Bond offerings and syndicated loan refinancings in my company.

The reason is that, in reality, the computer does all the calculation and I simply double-check whether the calculation is correct. Not until then did I realize that checking versus knowing how to calculate the bond interests and amortization is vastly different.

Toward the end of my FAR study, I was dead tired and wanted to give up, secretly hoping that these calculations would not appear on the exam. I was lucky that I got some time at the very end to really understand how the calculations worked. Both bonds and leases were heavily tested in my exam.

Lesson learned: Do not skip the difficult concepts and hope they will not appear on the exam. Plan ahead for sufficient time to cover everything so you can take the exam with confidence.

Spend Less Time Reading and More Time Practicing

Many readers emailed me about how they failed FAR. In most cases they ran out of the time because they spent a disproportionate amount of time reviewing the videos and concepts. Given that FAR is computation-heavy, more time should be spent on practice questions. After a change in study strategies, many of my readers were able to pass on their second attempt.

Do Not Give Up Governmental Accounting

I was overwhelmed by the section on governmental accounting because I never learned it in school and I have never dealt with it in real life—the rules simply did not make much sense to me. It was not until I spent a full day analyzing how the calculations work that things started to click. If you are a nonaccounting major or the governmental accounting rules are different in your country, set aside extra time for this section.

Governmental accounting represents 8 to 12 percent of the exam content. Although the percentage is smaller than other topics, if you give up and lose 8 to 12 points, your chance of passing FAR will be much lower.

The same applies to other topics that you may find too complex to deal with in this section. If you get stuck, ask for help. You can do it!

Presenting the Outline

You find below the outline of the FAR exam content as well as suggestions on how to approach the review materials. The outline is written based on the *Wiley CPA Exam Review* but the tips are applicable to other review courses.

Module 9: Basic Theory and Financial Reporting

This is one of the few conceptual topics you will find in the FAR exam. International candidates may need to pay special attention to the format of these U.S. generally accepted accounting principles (GAAP) financial statements, which can be quite different from the ones commonly used in your country.

Basic Concepts

We begin the study with a conceptual discussion of basic accounting theory, definition of financial reporting, and components of the conceptual framework for financial accounting and reporting, accruals and deferrals, cash to accrual, installment sales, and other types of revenue recognition. You can read through the pages without memorizing the details.

Error Correction

This section discusses the errors commonly found in financial statements and how they can be corrected. For the purpose of the exam, it is important to read the question carefully. The examiners may be asking for the effects of error versus correction of the error—the difference in one word changes the entire meaning of the question. Other frequently asked questions include finding the amount of over/understatement in the financial statements.

Accounting Changes

This section focuses primarily on the changes in:

- Accounting principles
- Accounting estimates
- Reporting entities

You may want to study the example for each of the accounting changes to consolidate your understanding of the concepts. There is also a brief discussion on how International Financial Reporting Standards (IFRS) account for accounting changes.

Financial Statements

This section goes over the format of balance sheets as well as the income and retained earnings statements. It also discusses how unusual or infrequent items, discontinued operations, and comprehensive income should be presented in the financial statement.

There are further discussions on comparative financial statements, prospective financial information, and SEC reporting requirements.

Module 10: Inventory

If you have some knowledge of financial accounting, this is a breeze. Do not dwell on this topic for too long because you want to spend more time on the tougher modules such as bonds, pensions, stockholders' equity, and governmental accounting.

Determining Inventory and Cost of Goods Sold

This module begins with a conceptual discussion of inventory cost as a function of the number of units in the inventory and the costs of those units. It also covers the different recording of inventory and cost of goods sold using the periodic system and perpetual system. Time should be spent on studying the journal entries presented in the review materials.

Inventory Valuation and Cost-Flow Methods

This section covers the many methods of inventory valuation including specific identification, weighted average, simple average, moving average, lower of cost or market, losses on purchase commitment, "First In, First Out" (FIFO), "Last In, First Out" (LIFO), and a few others.

In the CPA exam, you may see a question with a given scenario. You will need to apply the best inventory valuation and perform the calculation.

Items to Include in Inventory

Whether the goods are shipped FOB shipping point and are in transit, or whether they are shipped FOB destination affects the treatment of inventory. The former should be included in the inventory of the buyer, and the latter in the inventory of the seller until the goods reach the buyer.

Consignments

Consigned goods remain the property of the consignor (producer of the goods) until sold. The consignor can recognize the revenue only when the consignee (sale agent) sells the goods to the customer.

Ratios

Ratios related to inventory are:

- Inventory turnover: Cost of goods sold divided by average inventory.
- Number of days' supply in average inventory: 365 divided by inventory turnover.

Long-Term Construction Contracts

There are two ways to account for long-term contracts:

1. Completed-contract method
2. Percentage-of-completion method

Under the completed-contract method, contract revenue and profit are recognized at the point of completion. Cost is deferred based on the matching principle. Under the percentage-of-completion method, contract revenue and profit are recognized based on the estimated percentage of completed work. Costs are recognized in the period in which they occur. This method can only be used when the progress can be reasonably estimated.

Candidates will be asked to pick the preferred method based on a fact situation and perform the calculation accordingly. Therefore, you should understand not only the calculation but also the advantages and disadvantages of these two methods.

International Financial Reporting Standards

IFRS accounts for inventory differently mostly in these three areas:

1. LIFO cost flow assumption is not permitted.
2. Inventories are carried at the lower of cost or net realizable value.
3. In U.S. GAAP, interest cost cannot be capitalized as an inventory cost. In IFRS, this is generally the case except in the situation where it takes a long time to prepare the goods for sale in the production process.

Module 11: Fixed Assets

Similar to the previous module on inventory, you should move on once you understand 80 to 90 percent of the materials.

Acquisition Cost

The key to this section is to understand the matching principle: The cost associated with the purchase of the fixed asset is deferred to future periods based on the useful life of the asset. It is also important to include all necessary costs. For example, the cost of a new building should include the cost of demolishing the old building on the same site, direct materials and labor costs, variable overhead, and a fair share of fixed overhead cost.

Capitalization of Interest

Whether the interest cost can be capitalized depends on the preparation time of the asset. If the asset is purchased (no preparation time for the purchaser), interest cost cannot be capitalized; for a self-constructed fixed asset that takes considerable time to build, then the interest cost can be capitalized. Candidates should know how to determine the interest rate and interest capitalization period.

Nonmonetary Exchanges

This section goes over the definition, treatment, and recording of nonmonetary exchanges. The assets involved are mostly recorded at fair value. Book value is used if fair value cannot be determined.

Purchase of Groups of Fixed Assets

Cost should be allocated based on relative market value.

Capital versus Revenue Expenditures

This section goes over the difference between capital and revenue expenditures and their appropriate accounting treatment.

Depreciation

Depreciation is the spreading of cost over the useful life of the assets based on the matching principle. There are two types of depreciation: straight-line and accelerated depreciation. Candidates will be asked when and how these two different methods are applied. Other depreciation methods such as inventory depreciation and composite depreciation are discussed.

Disposals and Impairment of Value

This section presents the accounting entries related to disposal and impairment of assets. The focus should be on how depreciation, accumulated depreciation, and gain and loss are accounted for in each scenario.

Goodwill and Other Tangible Assets

Goodwill is an important concept that you need to master for business combination (Module 18). This section discusses in detail the acquisition, allocation, amortization, and impairment of intangible assets, with special coverage on goodwill.

Other Miscellaneous Topics

- **Depletion**: You need to know the recording of depletion and calculation of depletion rate.
- **Insurance**: Discussion on loss accounts for fixed assets.
- **Reporting on the costs of start-up activities**: These are one-off items and should be expensed as incurred.
- **Research and development costs**: Mostly expensed as incurred with a few exceptions.
- **Computer software costs**: There are two criteria for software to be considered for internal use. Cost can be capitalized if criteria are met.
- **Development stage enterprises**: These are companies at the beginning stage of setting up a new business. Necessary disclosure is required on financial statements.

International Financial Reporting Standards

Candidates should pay special attention to the IFRS rule on fixed assets because this is where a significant difference from U.S. GAAP can be found. Review the materials concerning the IFRS accounting treatment of plant, property, and equipment, investment property, intangible assets, and impairment of assets.

Module 12: Monetary Current Assets and Current Liabilities

This is another relatively easy topic. You will likely score well if you have a good understanding of balance sheet items.

Cash

This module begins with a brief discussion of cash, cash equivalents, and special cash funds, as well as the treatment of restricted cash and petty cash.

Receivables

This section focuses on the recognition of account receivables under the following scenarios:

- Anticipation of sales discount.
- Bad debt expense, under both the direct write-off method or allowance method.
- Transfers and servicing of financial assets such as securitization, factoring, and transfers of receivable with recourse.

Current Liabilities

This section introduces the different types of current liabilities and focuses on the definition, recording, and disclosure of contingencies.

Fair Value Option

This is a brief discussion on how the fair value option can be used.

Ratios

Ratios for Measuring Short-Term Viability

- Acid-test ratio
- Current ratio

Ratios for Measuring Operational Efficiency

- Receivable turnover
- Number of days' sales in average receivables
- Inventory turnover

- Number of days' supply in average inventory
- Length of operating cycle

International Financial Reporting Standards

IFRS accounts for current assets and current liabilities differently in the following areas:

- The different treatment of short-term obligation to be refinanced: It is grouped under noncurrent liability in U.S. GAAP but is mostly grouped under current liability in IFRS.
- The terminologies and rules on the provisions and contingencies are different between the two standards. Refer to the review materials for a detailed explanation.

Module 13: Present Value

This is a challenging module for many candidates: The concepts are complicated and questions often involve long and tedious calculations. I recommend that you set aside a longer period of study because it takes time to go through the concept and calculation even for one question. If possible, start studying with this module first to minimize the risk of running out of time. You cannot pass FAR without a good understanding of present value, bonds, and pensions.

Fundamentals

This section goes over the definition and the most commonly used application of the following concepts on the time value of money:

- Future value (FV) of an amount.
- Present value (PV) of a future amount.
- Compounding.
- Future value of an ordinary annuity.
- Present value of an ordinary annuity.

You are not expected to perform the complex calculation for the time value of money factor (TVMF). Instead, you will be given a TVMF table and will be asked to pick the correct percentage to complete the calculation.

Note

You may have studied present value in finance classes or in preparation for other professional exams. In most cases you can easily get the answer by using the scientific calculator. In the CPA exam, however, you are given only the basic calculator on the screen and you will have to know how to look up the TVMF table.

Bonds

This is a discussion on bonds payable and bond investments, including:

- Accounting treatment for both the issuer and the investor.
- Effective interest versus straight-line amortization methods.
- Valuation and recording of convertible bonds.
- Debt issued with detachable purchase warrants.
- Extinguishment of debt.

Allow sufficient time to study each example in detail and take advantage of the numerous practice questions available in this section.

Debt Restructure

There are two types of debt restructure: settlement of debt and modification of terms. This section discusses the impact on creditors and debtors under each scenario and the corresponding accounting entries.

Pensions

This section goes over the difference between a "defined contribution pension plan" and "defined benefit pension plan" and the corresponding accounting entries. For defined benefit pension plans, there is further discussion on the calculation and reporting of net pension asset and liability.

Note

Pension is a difficult subject for many candidates, especially for those with international backgrounds. This topic includes key terms that are confusingly similar and used only in the U.S. pension system. You may need to spend additional time to understand and memorize the meaning of the terminologies.

Leases

This section goes over the two types of leases—operating lease and capital lease—focusing on the calculation and recording for the lessor and lessee. Candidates are expected to complete the journal entries and apply the correct lease calculations based on various fact situations.

Leases are widely used in our daily lives but if you do not have an accounting background, the calculations can appear complex and difficult to understand. Take sufficient time to work through the examples and practice questions.

Module 14: Deferred Taxes

This module can seem intimidating at first but the concept is relatively straightforward once you understand permanent difference versus temporary difference. The calculations tend to take a longer time to complete. It is best if you can set aside a longer study time for this section.

Deferred tax results from the difference between income for tax purposes and income for financial reporting purposes. One key concept is the permanent difference and temporary difference—deferred tax is recognized only in the case of temporary difference.

Other topics in this section include the calculation and recording of deferred tax assets and liabilities, loss carry forwards and loss carryback, and the components in continuing operations, other comprehensive income, and retained earnings.

A notable difference between the U.S. GAAP and IFRS is the classification of deferred taxes on the balance sheet. Refer to the review materials for details.

Module 15: Stockholders' Equity

This is a long module covering many topics. It is likely that you are not familiar with at least some of the tested areas and therefore it is worth spending more time on this section. Stockholders' equity is closely related to many items in the financial statement. Once you understand the flow of accounting entries and the resulting calculation, you will most likely do better in other tested areas in FAR.

Common Stock

This section lists the accounting entries of:

- Common stock issuance.
- Setting up a control account for unissued stock.
- Treatment of no-par stock.
- How the costs of registering and issuing common stock (mostly legal expenses) are netted against the proceeds in the form of reduction in paid-in capital in excess of par.

Preferred Stock

Preferred stockholders have the right to receive dividends prior to common stockholders. Candidates should understand the basic definition and the meaning of participating, cumulative, convertible, and callable preferred stocks.

Stock Subscriptions

This section shows the journal entries in various stages of stock subscription. First, a subscription receivable account is set up and stock subscribed is credited. Upon cash receipt and issuance of stock, stock subscribed is debited and common stock is credited. There is also a discussion related to the default on the subscription agreements.

Treasury Stock Transactions

Treasury stock is a company's own stock after being repurchased from the open market. It is treated as a reduction of stockholders' equity (instead of an asset). Candidates should understand the two accounting treatments—cost method and par value method.

Dividends

Candidates should understand the recording of dividends from the date of declaration to the payment date using journal entries, as well as the meaning of property dividends, liquidation dividends, strip dividends, and stock dividends.

Other Topics on Stocks

- **Retirement of stock:** Treated similarly to treasury stock.
- **Stock splits:** A corporate action of changing the number of shares outstanding and the par value of shares. Since the total par value does not change, retained earnings remain the same.
- **Appropriations of retained earnings:** Also known as the *reserves*, it is used to restrict the amount of retained earnings available for dividends.
- **Share-based payment:** Refers to payments for goods and services by issuing shares, share options, and other equity instruments. Share-based payments to nonemployees are measured at the fair value of the goods and services or that of the equity instruments, whichever is more reliable. Share-based payments to employees are measured on a fair-value-based method.

Basic Earnings per Share

Earnings per share (EPS) disclosure is mandatory for public companies and optional for nonpublic companies. To compute the EPS, candidates should know how to calculate the net income from continuing operations.

Diluted Earnings per Share

Diluted earnings per share is EPS with the consideration of all dilutive potential common shares outstanding, such as options and warrants, convertible bonds, and preferred stock.

Candidates who are not familiar with the various financial instruments may be intimidated by the complexity of the calculation. Once you understand how each of these instruments can be converted into common stock, the rest of the calculation is straightforward.

Bankruptcy and Reorganizations

Corporate Bankruptcy   You should know the prioritization of equity inter-ests in the event of a corporate bankruptcy, and how a "statement of affairs" is presented based on the balance sheet upon bankruptcy. You may want to refer to Module 30, "Bankruptcy," in the next chap-ter for a review on the legal and regulatory perspective.

Reorganizations   There is a discussion on reporting of financial state-ments in the event of Chapter 11 reorganization. A basic under-standing is sufficient for the purpose of the FAR exam.

Quasi Reorganization   Quasi reorganization allows companies to undergo steps similar to reorganization through an informal proceeding. The procedure includes seeking the authority from stockholders and creditors, revaluation of assets to current values, and elimination of deficit by charging paid-in capital.

Other Miscellaneous Topics

Stock Rights   There is a brief discussion on how stock rights are handled. An accounting entry is made only upon exercising the rights.

Employee Stock Ownership Plan (ESOP)   ESOP is a stock bonus plan that invests primarily in employer securities. On the balance sheet, ESOP is credited as a liability and debited as a reduction in shareholders' equity.

Ratios

Candidates should memorize these formulas:

- Dividend payout ratio
- Book value of common stock
- Return on common stockholders' equity
- Debt to equity ratio

Module 16: Investments

This module goes over the recognition, measurement, valuation, cal-culation, presentation, and disclosures of investments. It is more of a conceptual topic that ties in with other challenging sections such as consolidation of financial statements.

Concepts of Accounting and Investment Percentage

This section discusses the two main classifications of investments:

1. Investment in debt securities: trading securities, available-for-sale securities, and held-to-maturity securities.
2. Investment in equity securities: accounting rules vary based on the percentage of voting stock obtained and the extent of influence the investor has on the investee.

Investments in Which Significant Influence Does Not Exist

This applies to investment in the form of debt securities and equity securities with less than 20 percent ownership. Note that the 20 percent level is indicative—a different accounting treatment should be used whenever the investor has significant influence on the investee. Candidates should have a good understanding of how the investment is reported on the balance sheet, and how realized and unrealized gains and losses are reported on the income statement.

Investments Where Significant Influences Does Exist

The equity method is to be used when the investor can exercise significant influence on the investee. This is typically the case when the investor owns 20 to 50 percent of the investee. In the case where the investor's influence is temporary, the cost adjusted for fair value method should be used. You are expected to perform a full calculation using the equity method in the CPA exam.

Other Miscellaneous Topics

- **Equity method and deferred income taxes:** Recognition of deferred taxes may be required when the equity method is used.
- **The fair value option:** This section discusses when and how an entity may elect to value its securities at fair value.
- **Stock dividends and splits:** Not recorded as income for the investor.
- **Stock rights:** This section discusses the nature of stock rights and its implication, such as the possible dilution of

investor ownership. Candidates should know the accounting entries related to the receipt, exercising, and lapsing of the rights.

- **Cash surrender of life insurance:** Considered a noncurrent investment when the company (versus employees) is the beneficiary.

International Financial Reporting Standards

There is no significant difference of treatment between U.S. GAAP and IFRS for investment, but you may want to familiarize yourself with the terms more commonly used in IFRS.

Module 17: Statement of Cash Flows

This module is moderately easy for candidates with knowledge in financial accounting. You can quickly go through the reading materials and spend most of the time on practice questions.

Objectives of the Statement of Cash Flows

The primary objective of this statement is to provide information on the entity's cash receipts and payments, as well as the financing and investing activities of the company.

Statement of Cash Flows Classifications

The statement of cash flows is presented in three categories: operational activities, investing activities, and financing activities such that users of the statement can determine whether the entity can:

- Generate positive cash flow from its operation.
- Manage the acquisition and deposition of long-term productive assets or securities.
- Meet its financial obligation and pay dividends.

You may want to study a sample statement of cash flows in detail and understand whether each item leads to positive or negative cash flow.

Direct or Indirect Presentation in Reporting Operating Activities

Direct presentation is preferred by FASB but indirect presentation is also permitted. A detailed example showing the reconciliation is presented in the review materials and you should take the time to study all the accounting entries.

Capital Leases

This is a brief discussion on how capital leases are accounted for in the statement of cash flow in both the direct and indirect method.

International Financial Reporting Standards

The accounting rules of the two standards are similar but certain items are presented differently on the statement of cash flows.

Module 18: Business Combinations and Consolidations

Business combination involves multiple steps in calculation, which tend to be complex, tedious, and time-consuming. If you do not have prior knowledge in this topic, you may want to spend half a day studying the examples and working through the computation one step at a time before attempting the practice questions.

Scope and Effective Dates for SFAS 141 (R)

This section defines the scope and introduces terminologies related to business combination, such as acquirer, acquiree, acquisition date, and control.

The Acquisition Method for Business Combinations

This section goes over the steps of business combination using the acquisition method:

- Identification of the acquirer
- Identification of acquisition date
- Recognition and measurement of identifiable assets, liability, and noncontrolling interest
- Recognition of goodwill

There is also a brief discussion on step acquisition, noncontrolling interest, and acquisition-related costs, and how they should be accounted for in the financial statements.

Consolidated Financial Statements

Consolidated financial statements are to be prepared when the acquirer obtains 50 percent or more of the outstanding voting stock and gains control of the acquiree. There is also a discussion on acquisitions concerning the variable interest entities (special-purpose entities).

In most CPA review courses you will find a complete case study of a business combination. Go through how the consolidated financial statements are prepared and how the adjustments and eliminations are done.

Consolidated Financial Statement Subsequent to Acquisition

The concept is the same as the consolidated financial statement prepared at the acquisition date, but additional steps (such as elimination due to intercompany transactions) may be required.

Intercompany Transactions and Profit Confirmation

There are three common types of intercompany transactions between the acquirer and acquiree:

1. Intercompany sales of merchandise
2. Intercompany fixed asset transactions
3. Intercompany bond transactions

Candidates should understand the treatment of unrealized profit and determine whether any gain or loss should be eliminated in the consolidated financial statements.

Noncontrolling Interest

In the case where the acquisition is less than 100 percent of the interest, the noncontrolling interest should be accounted for with adjustments in the income statement, retained earnings, and balance sheet.

Additional Issues Regarding Business Combination

This section discusses miscellaneous items including incomplete information, transfer of assets, contingent considerations, and recognition of exceptional items such as leases, income taxes, and employee benefits. These items are relatively less important in the context of the CPA exam.

Additional Disclosures

You will find a list of items that should be disclosed in the notes to the financial statements. You can skim through the list without the need to memorize the content.

Combined Financial Statements

Combined financial statements are prepared for companies that are owned by the same parent company, and intercompany transactions, balances, profit, and loss are eliminated as in the consolidated statements. Note that this statement is not related to business combination and should not to be confused with consolidated financial statements.

Push-Down Accounting

Push-down accounting is applicable when a large and wholly (or substantially) owned subsidiary prepares a separate financial statement. You can read the details on how and why push-down accounting is used in the review materials.

International Financial Reporting Standards

Under IFRS, business combination is also accounted for by using the acquisition method. There are, however, notable differences in the treatment of noncontrolling interest and the use of push-down accounting. The definition of whether the parent has control (and thus whether consolidated financial statement should be used) is also different between the two standards.

Module 19: Derivative Instruments and Hedging Activities

This module provides an introduction to foreign currency transactions and derivative instruments. You will likely see questions in the introductory level only. There may be some calculations involving foreign currency transactions.

Foreign Currency Transactions

If the company pays or receives in non-U.S. dollars, it is exposed to foreign currency risk and may need to recognize the gain or loss in the income statement. You should read more examples on how foreign currency can impact other financial statements such as the balance sheet.

Derivative Instruments and Hedging Activities

This section introduces the various derivative instruments. These instruments are measured and reported at fair value. You will also find a useful list of items that are included or excluded in the definition of derivative instruments. Candidates should also take the time to understand the three types of hedges: fair value hedge, cash flow hedge, and foreign currency hedge.

International Financial Reporting Standards

The concepts of the two standards are similar. You may want to read the brief discussion on IFRS rules on derivatives in the review materials.

Module 20: Miscellaneous

Personal Financial Statements (PFS)

Personal financial statements are prepared for individuals and consist of:

- Statements of financial condition.
- Statements of changes in net worth.

Accrual basis of accounting should be used. Candidates are expected to know how the assets and liabilities are valued for PFS.

Interim Reporting

Interim reporting is a type of financial reporting prepared for periods of less than one year, typically on a quarterly basis. Interim reporting generally follows the rules of that for annual reporting but you can go over the few exceptions in the review materials.

Segment Reporting

Segment reporting provides additional information on the operation for investors and lenders. Financial data is typically segmented in terms of products and services, geographical areas, and major customers.

Partnership Accounting

This section discusses the formation of a partnership, allocation of partnership income, and the treatment in the event of a change in ownership, withdrawal, and transactions between a partner and the partnership.

Foreign Currency Translation

When considering the currency translation of foreign entities, you should first identify the functional currency, then translate the items into the functional currency, and finally translate the items into the presentation currency. Do not expect that the functional currency must be the U.S. dollar or the local currency of the foreign country—it should be the currency of the primary economic environment in which the entity operates.

Module 21: Government (State and Local) Accounting

It is fair to say that government accountancy is the one of the biggest beasts in FAR. Candidates rarely have working knowledge in this area and many have never taken a related course at school. Therefore, you should pay special attention to this topic. Government accounting represents around 10 percent of exam topics. Although it may not seem significant, it is too big to ignore for the purpose of this exam.

The Governmental Reporting Model

This is a conceptual discussion covering the requirements of governmental reporting and its focus on operational accountability and fiscal accountability.

The Reporting Entity

The reporting entity consists of:

- A primary government: A state government or a general-purpose local government.

- Appropriate component units: Legally separate organizations for which elected officials of a primary government are financially responsible.

Management's Discussion and Analysis (MD&A)

The purpose of MD&A in governmental accounting is similar to that used in the corporation—to provide an overview of the financial activities and comparison of results in current year versus prior year.

Government-Wide Financial Statements

The government-wide financial statements consist of the Statement of Net Assets and Statement of Activities, which are equivalent to balance sheet and income statement respectively.

Fund Financial Statements

Fund financial statements are typically used as a basis to prepare the government-wide statements. There are 11 fund types categorized into government funds, propriety funds, and fiduciary funds.

There is a lengthy discussion on each of the three fund categories. Allocate extra time to go through the pages, understand the concepts, and memorize the fund types.

Other Topics Related to the Statements

Government accounting is a huge topic. It is impossible to go over even the summary of the topics here. Find below the topics you will need to cover for this exam.

- Notes to the financial statements.
- Required supplementary information (RSI) other than MD&A.
- Measurement focus and basis of accounting (MFBA).
- Accounting by governments for certain events and transactions.
- Budgetary accounting for the general and special revenue funds.
- Expenditure classification for governmental funds.
- Accounting for the general fund.
- Accounting for special revenue fund.

- Accounting for capital projects fund.
- Debt service funds.
- Permanent funds.
- Accounting for special assessments.
- Accounting for proprietary funds.
- Accounting for fiduciary funds.
- Reporting interfund activity.
- Accounting for investments.
- Conversion from fund financial statements to government-wide financial statements.
- College and university accounting—public (governmental).

Note

It is most important that you know the components of government-wide financial statements and the fund financial statements, and how to convert the latter to the former. At the minimum, learn the basic concepts such as the fund types, basic entries, and conceptual requirements in order to get a decent score in this topic.

If the discussion does not make any sense, get a good night's sleep and read it again. Things may start to click when you review the materials again.

Module 22: Not-for-Profit Accounting

Not-for-profit accounting is another topic that could be completely new to you. The good news is that this module is less complicated than governmental accounting. I suggest that you take a quick look at the review materials, then spend sufficient time to work your way through the illustrative statements. You may want to work on the practice questions immediately afterward to consolidate your understanding of this topic.

FASB and AICPA Standards for Private Sector Nonprofits

This section goes over the important features of the FASB guideline on private sector not-for-profit organizations, and the required financial statements:

- Statement of financial position
- Statement of activities

- Statement of cash flows
- Statement of functional expenses (required only for voluntary health and welfare organizations)

Note

Similar to governmental accounting, the lengthy discussion can easily overwhelm any candidate. If this section is too much for you to handle, I suggest that you focus only on studying the first three financial statements and work on the practice questions to understand how they work. This can help you score enough points to pass the FAR exam.

College and University Accounting—Private Sector Institutions

The reporting is the same as above with a few exceptions. Focus on studying the examples and the accounting entries.

Health Care Organization Accounting—Private Sector

This section goes over the requirement of health care organization accounting for private sector. You can quickly go through the discussion and focus on studying the sample financial statements.

Health Care Organization Accounting—Governmental

This section focuses on how various guides and rules govern the reporting of health care organizations. Note that the AICPA health care guide should be used whenever possible. You can skim through the rest of the discussion when you have the time.

Readers' Sharing

You are going to spend a lot of time on this exam section, and you are not alone. I conclude this long chapter with this light-hearted email from one of my readers:

> Hi Stephanie, when I was studying the bonds on FAR, I had two weird dreams (or nightmares):

Dream 1 = I was a journal entry, i.e., a "Debit—Discount," and I was arguing with a "Bond payable"...

Dream 2 = I was practicing the formulas on Excel for the bonds, and I once dreamt that I was an Excel cell ...

I wasn't too worried about these dreams ... I guess it meant my brain was processing the info!

—Najet

Najet did pass FAR with a score of 82 on her first attempt.

12

Regulation (REG)

The Regulation exam section consists of two main topics: business ethics/law and taxation, accounting for approximately 35 percent and 65 percent respectively.

While both topics are relevant to the regulatory aspects of the accounting profession, they are drastically different in the context of the CPA exam. A tax accountant may find it easy to go over the tax section but may have a hard time memorizing the concepts in contracts and debtor-creditor relationship. On the other hand, an auditor is familiar with the legal responsibility of accountants but may spend many grueling hours studying the exclusions and itemized deductions.

For international candidates, REG is likely the biggest challenge because both business ethics/law and taxation could be new to you. I do not think you can skip any study modules and expect to pass, but you can follow my guide to study more effectively and aim to clear the exam on your first attempt.

What Does REG Cover?

Here is the examination specification released by the American Institute of Certified Public Accountants (AICPA):

- Ethics, professional, and legal responsibilities (15 to 19 percent)
- Business law (17 to 21 percent)

- Federal tax process, procedures, accounting, and planning (11 to to 15 percent)
- Federal taxation of property transactions (12 to 16 percent)
- Federal taxation of individuals (13 to 19 percent)
- Federal taxation of entities (18 to 24 percent)

This is a three-hour examination, with three testlets each containing 24 multiple-choice questions and one testlet containing six task-based simulation questions. The multiple-choice questions are adaptive but the simulations are not.

Passing Rate History and Trend

The passing rate in 1Q 2005 was a chilling 35 percent (Figure 12.1). Since then, the percentage has been steadily increasing to around 50 percent. The passing rate in 2012 was 48.2 percent.

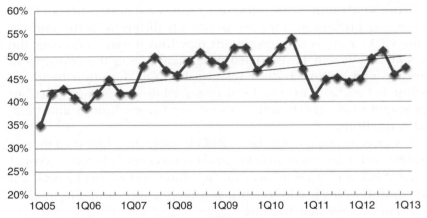

Figure 12.1   REG Exam Passing Rate Trend, 2005–2012

Source: www.aicpa.org.

Study and Exam-Taking Tips

I go over the tips in each study module in greater detail. Here are some suggestions for your reference.

Straddle the Taxation Study Modules with Lighter Topics

I personally find business law and ethics easier to handle. When preparing for my own CPA exam, I gave myself a "treat" of studying the business law/ethics whenever I finished reviewing a section of the taxation module. If you are a tax accountant, you might want to do the reverse.

Work on the Terminology First in Business Law

Some of you may find business law impossible—the terms and the rules can be very confusing. If this applies to you, I suggest tackling the legal terminology first. Business law is intuitive once you overcome the fear of the "big words."

Do Not Underestimate Ethics

Business ethics has become more important in real life, so expect plenty of these in the exam. If ethics is your blind spot, then the best approach for you is to work on many practice tests until you understand the concepts inside out.

Time Yourself in the Exam

Many candidates run out of time in the REG exam, mostly because the task-based simulation section is very difficult and often involves tedious calculations. Try to work through the multiple-choice questions quickly and save more time for the last part of the exam.

Sims May Look Impossible, but You Will Likely Be Okay

Nine out of 10 readers told me they bombed in the task-based simulations and expected a fail, but at least half of them managed to pass. REG sims are meant to be long and complex. Don't panic; try your best.

Presenting the Outline

Below is the outline of the REG exam content as well as suggestions on how to approach the review materials. The outline is written based on the *Wiley CPA Exam Review* but the tips are applicable to other review courses.

Module 23: Professional and Legal Responsibilities

This module discusses the legal responsibilities and liabilities of an accountant, mostly in the perspective of public accounting.

Boards of Accountancy Regulations for Profession

This is a short section on the CPA license being granted by the boards of accountancy in various states and jurisdictions, and that the AICPA Code of Professional Conduct is applicable to all AICPA members regardless of whether the member is practicing in public accounting.

Disciplinary Systems of the Profession and State Regulatory Bodies

You will see the names of many professional and regulatory bodies. The abbreviations may look confusingly similar. The goal is to recognize the names together with the abbreviations without memorizing the minute details.

Accountants' Legal Liabilities

This section discusses accountants' legal liabilities:

- Common law liability to clients
- Common law liability to third parties
- Statutory liability to third parties related to the Securities Exchange Acts of 1933 and 1934

You should be able to tell whether an accountant is liable for a specific type of liability. For example, an accountant is liable for negligence but not liable for any failure to detect fraud.

Note

This is another way to test your concepts on the responsibility of the auditor covered in Audit and Attestation (AUD). It is useful to remember the situations where a CPA is liable to his or her clients and to third parties, and to what extent the illegal act is considered criminal.

Legal Considerations Affecting the Accountant's Responsibility

This section deals with how accountants handle the working paper and privileged communications with clients, as well as how confidentiality, privacy laws, and illegal acts of clients and employees may affect their practices.

The general rule is that:

- Accountants should keep client information confidential.
- Federal laws and some state laws do not recognize privileged communications between accountants and client.
- If an illegal act is discovered, the accountant is not liable but has the duty to notify relevant parties.

After understanding and remembering the basic rules, you can spend 5 to 10 minutes reading the exceptions listed on the book.

Criminal Liability

The key is not whether the act is illegal, but whether the accountant "willfully" or "intentionally" performs the illegal act directly or indirectly.

Responsibilities of Auditors under Private Securities Litigation Reform Act

The central idea is that auditors should establish procedures to detect material illegal acts and identify related-party transactions. Accountants may be held liable for the proportionate or even full share of damages they cause depending on circumstances. Read the examples to understand the damages at different levels.

Responsibilities under Sarbanes-Oxley Act

If you are not familiar with the Sarbanes-Oxley Act, it is worth the time to read through the background, including the creation of the Public Company Accounting Oversight Board (PCAOB) and the increased disclosure requirement for both the auditors and executive officers of public companies. Major points include:

- New federal laws make willful nonretention of audit and review work papers a criminal act.
- PCAOB regulates public accounting firms that audit Securities and Exchange Commission (SEC) registrants.
- SEC registrants (public companies) have additional responsibilities, including more disclosure related to executive officers.

- CEOs and CFOs of most large public companies are required to certify financial statements filed with the SEC.

The provisions of this Act are discussed more extensively in the next module (Module 24). Questions related to the Sarbanes-Oxley Act may also appear in other exam sections such as the BEC under corporate governance.

Additional Statutory Liability against Accountants

The reasoning is similar to the accountants' legal responsibility and liabilities. It is a good section to test your ability to get the correct answers based on logic instead of blind memorization.

Responsibilities of Tax Return Preparers

This section goes through the responsibilities, the AICPA standards, knowledge of error, and possible penalties of tax return preparers. The list is quite detailed but straightforward.

Module 24: Federal Securities Acts

This module discusses the important securities acts enacted in the United States. I list the main objective of each act. Spend the time to read over each of them.

Securities Act of 1933

At the minimum, you should know that the Act is related to:

- Initial issuance of securities.
- Disclosure of all material information by issuer.
- Protection of potential investors and prevention of fraud and misrepresentation.

You can start with reading the definition of keywords such as securities, controlling person, insider, and underwriter, then read the sections on registration requirements and possible exemptions. There is a fair amount of memorization. Here are a few tips:

- Think through how each point relates to the overall objective of this Act.

- Rewrite the review materials in summary form, either on flash cards or in the margins of your book.

Securities Exchange Act of 1934

This is similar to the 1933 Act except that it deals with subsequent trading of securities instead of initial issuance. Therefore, focus is on how the subsequent trading is regulated and how periodic disclosure is required.

Sarbanes-Oxley Act of 2002

This is a more detailed discussion on the provisions of this Act. Spend sufficient time to read over each point carefully.

Miscellaneous Topics

The rest of this module discusses the following short and lightly tested topics. You can allocate no more than five minutes for this part of study.

- **Internet Securities Offering (ISO)**: A quick discussion on the rationale behind this type of offering and how the offering is implemented.
- **Electronic Signatures and Electronic Records**: These records have the same legal effect as the nonelectronic versions.
- **State "Blue-Sky" Laws**: Each state may have its own laws that must be complied with in addition to federal laws.

Note

It is easy to mix up the details in these Acts. When working on the exam questions, keep in mind the main objective of the Act before answering the question. For example, there is a question on the details of the 1934 Act. You know that the 1934 Act relates to the subsequent trading of securities, and therefore any answer that mentions initial issuance of securities would be incorrect. You can use this method to eliminate most if not all incorrect answers without the need to memorize every detail of the provisions.

Module 25: Business Structure

This module discusses sole proprietorships, partnerships, and corporations as well as other related business organizations. Focus of study should be on the basic understanding of the three major structures, the differences among them, and the advantages and disadvantages of each.

Nature of Sole Proprietorships

This is most likely covered in the introductory business or economics class that you have taken. Review is required only if you graduated a long time ago and need some reminders on the main points.

Nature of Partnerships

Partnerships are more complicated as there are contractual and fiduciary relationships between partners. It also touches the concept of agency as each partner is considered an agent.

Take the time to study the rules related to:

- Formation of partnership
- Partners' rights
- Relationship to third parties (principle-agent relationships)
- Termination of partnerships

You can expect some computations on how profits and losses are split among the partners.

Corporations

Similar to partnerships, take the time to go through the types of corporations, formation, structure, liabilities, rights and liability of stockholders, and substantial change in corporate structure.

Special attention should be paid to the structure of the corporation. You are expected to know the details of the different types of stocks (e.g., issued stocks, unissued stocks, treasury stock, par-value stock) and other related terminologies. Also read carefully about the stockholders' rights and liabilities.

Other Business Structures

There are discussions on limited partnerships, joint ventures, limited liability companies (LLC), limited liability partnerships (LLP),

Subchapter C corporations, and Subchapter S corporations. You are expected to know the difference and the rationale behind the choice of a particular business structure.

Note

Expect some computational questions involving the operations of business, such as the amount of capital contribution for each partner, or the proportion of stock a stockholder is allowed to buy in a new issuance. The calculation is often simple but you have to understand the underlying concepts to get the correct answers.

Module 26: Contracts

This is a typical business law module. It could be time-consuming to read over all the details, but if you understand the logic and remember what the keywords mean, you will likely score well in this subject.

Essential Elements of a Contract

This is an overview of the terminologies you will find in contract laws.

Types of Contracts

This is another quick overview of the different types of contracts. Typically the name of the term suggests the characteristics. For example, an "express contract" refers to one with terms specifically "expressed" orally or in writing.

Discussion of Essential Elements of a Contract

If your work involves reviewing of legal documents, you can skip this section. For international candidates who may not be familiar with these terms in English, you may want to allocate extra time to understand and remember how the terms can be used.

Assignment and Delegation

This is a more in-depth discussion on the meaning of assignment and delegation. You can learn more efficiently by focusing on the examples.

Third-Party Beneficiary Contracts

This section goes over terms such as creditor beneficiary, donee beneficiary, and incidental beneficiary. Similar to the above, you can learn how the terms are used in the numerous examples presented in this section.

Performance of Contract

You will need to get familiar with terms such as "condition precedent," "condition subsequent," "tender of performance," and "doctrine of substantial performance."

> **Note**
>
> There are many big words with simple meanings in this module. It is useful to write down the terms on one side of the flash card and the meaning on the other side, and flip through these cards whenever you have a few minutes of idle time.

Discharge of Contracts

This section discusses the various situations where the parties want to break out of the contract of agreement, such as breach of contract or other reasons (e.g., bankruptcy). Get familiar with related terminologies such as mutual rescission and novation.

Remedies

The most common remedy under contract law is to provide an actual or compensatory damage equivalent to the amount caused by the breach. This section goes over other types of remedies and the respective rules under contract law.

Miscellaneous Topics

The rest of the review goes through the concept of statute of limitations, how the court generally rules regarding the jurisdiction over a defendant for online transactions, and the rule in the case of interference with contractual relations.

Module 27: Sales

This is another module that takes time to read but is not difficult. You can move on after understanding 80 to 90 percent of the content.

Contracts for Sale of Goods

This module begins with the definition of *goods*, which generally refers to tangible properties and not the sales of investment securities, accounts receivables, contract rights, copyrights, and patents.

The Uniform Commercial Code (UCC) governs the contract for the sale of goods. It is helpful to know that the UCC adopts most of the common law rules for contracts.

Product Liability

The seller or manufacturer is responsible when the goods are defective or cause injuries or damages. The three types of product liabilities are:

1. Warranty liability—Goods different from what is "promised" in the warranty.
2. Negligence—Manufacturer or seller do not exercise reasonable care when producing or selling the goods.
3. Strict product liability—Defective goods.

Transfer of Property Rights

This section discusses the rules governing how a person acquires a property right (as known as title) of the goods and transfers this right to a third party.

Risk of Loss and Title

The bearer of the risk of loss can be agreed on by the parties beforehand. If an agreement is not available, UCC rules apply. Application of the UCC rules in this area includes the shipment contract, destination contract, and trial sales. There is also a discussion on rules regarding selling or shipping nonconforming goods and breaching the contracts.

Performance and Remedies under Sales Law

This section discusses the remedies of both the seller and buyer in the event of a breach of contract. Since this generally follows common sense, you can skim through the pages and study how the rules apply using the practice questions.

Leases under UCC

This section focuses on how the UCC rules govern leases. A basic understanding is sufficient for the purpose of the exam.

Contracts for the International Sales of Goods (CISG)

CISG is the contract of sales of goods between persons/companies of different countries. Another set of laws is necessary in addition to UCC because the United States has special treaties with different countries, particularly with countries in the Americas and Europe.

CISG has priority over UCC. The major differences can be found in price terms, time the contract is formed, acceptances, irrevocable offers, and written contracts. Refer to the review materials for details.

Module 28: Commercial Paper

Commercial paper (i.e., drafts, checks, and promissory notes) are commonly used in daily lives. You should know most of the rationale behind the many rules covered in this module. Candidates who run out of time for study may consider skipping the review and tackling the practice questions directly.

I consider this module a light reading that you can choose to study when you need a break from tougher sections, such as taxation discussed in later modules. Pay special attention to the concept of Holder in Due Course (HDC).

General Concepts of Commercial Paper

This topic discusses the functions of commercial paper such as a check or a promissory note, the difference between negotiable and nonnegotiable instrument. This short and straightforward section aims to give you an overview of this particular instrument.

Types of Commercial Paper

This section covers the difference between a draft (which includes checks) and a note, a simple concept that you can easily read within five minutes.

Requirements of Negotiability

While many points are common sense, it takes me a long time to pick the correct answers based only on reasoning. I personally find it easier to memorize the list of requirements.

Interpretation of Ambiguities in Negotiable Instruments

This topic covers how we handle commercial paper in the case of contradictory terms, omissions, and issues with the date (postdated or antedated). You probably know most if not all of these rules from everyday life.

Negotiation

The implementation of transfer and endorsement of commercial paper is discussed here. You can learn best by going through the many examples in this section.

Holder in Due Course (HDC)

This is an important topic and it ties in with the concept of contract rights. You need to know how a person can be qualified as an HDC under different scenarios.

Take sufficient time to carefully go through the concept. It is also a good idea to work on a few practice questions immediately after the review to consolidate your understanding.

Rights of a Holder in Due Course

The central theme is that a transfer of a negotiable instrument to an HDC cuts off all personal defenses (such as breach of contract) against the HDC. There are numerous rights covered in the review but you can tackle each one by understanding the examples.

Liability of Parties

This section explains who is responsible for paying the HDC, particularly whether the primary parties and/or the secondary parties are responsible. You will need a solid understanding of both the definition and the rights of HDC to answer these questions.

Other Miscellaneous Topics

You can skim through the following topics for background knowledge.

Banks A quick overview of a bank's function and its relationship with the depositor (debtor-creditor relationship) and the handling of checks.

Electronic Fund Transfer Act and Regulation E This subsection goes over the rules specific to electronic fund transfer in the United States. This is not an important topic, but international candidates may want to skim through this section before attempting the questions.

Fund Transfers under UCC Article 4A This applies to commercial electronic fund transfers.

Agencies Involved in Banking

The name of the following agencies may come up as part of the exam questions. International candidates may want to take extra time to remember the names and their major functions:

- Federal Reserve.
- FDIC: Insurer of customer deposits against bank failure.
- OCC: Arm of Treasury Department.
- CFTC: U.S. agency for monitoring the futures market.
- OTS: Enforces regulation governing the U.S. savings and loan industry.

Module 29: Secured Transactions

This is another module with many applications in daily lives. The focus is to understand the concepts of attachment and perfection of secured transactions, and the rules on priorities when several parties compete to claim the collateral. Pay special attention to the concepts of attachment, perfection, and PMSI.

Scope of Secured Transactions

The module begins with an overview of secured transactions and related parties (debtor, security interest, and security agreement) and the types of collateral in the form of goods, indispensible paper, and intangibles.

Attachment of Security Interests

This section discusses various situations when the security interest is "attached," or becomes enforceable against a debtor. This is a simple but important concept in this module. Attachment focuses on the rights between debtors and creditors.

Perfecting a Security Interest

Perfecting is an action to give the secured party priority over others who may claim the collateral. You need to distinguish the different types of perfection and understand when a security interest is considered PMSI.

Other Issues under Secured Transactions

This section discusses a few special cases such as security interests in goods acquired in the future and consignment.

Priorities

There are rules to follow when several parties claim a security interest in the same collateral. It is important for you to go through and memorize the sequence.

Rights of Parties upon Default

This is a related discussion on priorities in the case of a default. The logic is similar to the above but you may want to read how the collateral can be treated in this scenario.

Module 30: Bankruptcy

Bankruptcy is a hot topic in the business and financial community in recent years in light of the continuing debates on the merits of Chapter 11 reorganizations and soaring bankruptcy fees. You should therefore expect to see a fair amount of questions from this module.

Alternatives to Bankruptcy Proceedings

Alternative proceedings include receiverships and agreements between debtor and creditors to avoid bankruptcy. These are discussed in more detail in Module 31.

Bankruptcy in General

This is an overview of the concept of bankruptcy: to protect creditors' rights and at the same time allow debtors a fresh start free of previous debt. In the United States, there are three types of bankruptcy:

1. Chapter 7: Liquidation
2. Chapter 11: Reorganization of debts
3. Chapter 13: Reorganization of debts primarily for individuals

Note

International candidates may want to know that Chapter 7 bankruptcy proceedings are equivalent to the liquidation proceedings in your country.

Chapter 7 Voluntary Bankruptcy Petitions

This section discusses how a debtor can file a formal request for an order of relief. In the exam questions you might be asked to identify a voluntary bankruptcy petition based on various fact situations.

Chapter 7 Involuntary Bankruptcy Petitions

This is the case when creditors, instead of the debtor, initiate the petition to file with the bankruptcy court. You need to remember the details of the rules and be able to distinguish between voluntary and involuntary petitions.

Chapter 7 Bankruptcy Proceedings

You might be asked whether a property is included as part of the estate under different fact situations. You might also be asked about the Bankruptcy Code exemptions but there is no need to memorize the dollar amount. There might be questions on the role of trustees in bankruptcy proceedings.

Claims

This is a discussion on the types of claims, when the claims must be filed, and necessary proof of claims. This is a short and straightforward section that can be dealt with using common sense.

Priority of Claims

The priority of secured creditors and unsecured creditors is covered in this section. The priority is based first on domestic support obligation (e.g., child care) followed by the administration cost related to the bankruptcy, then by the ordinary course of the debtor's business, taxes, and other obligations. Refer to the review materials for a more detailed list.

Debts Not Discharged by Bankruptcy

The debtor is discharged of all debts not paid in bankruptcy (except the ones below), subject to improper action during bankruptcy proceedings, such as making false claims and refusing to obey court orders. In most cases you can answer these questions without the need to go over the review materials.

Debts not discharged by bankruptcy include:

- Taxes (including loans for tax payment) within three years of filing bankruptcy petition.
- Government dues.
- Domestic support obligation, for example, child support and alimony.
- Liability due to wrongful and illegal acts, for example, fraud, theft, embezzlement, and intentional torts.

You can get a more detailed list in the review materials. There are also rules targeting the abuse of discharging student loans upon bankruptcy and the practice of loading up on luxury goods before bankruptcy.

Revocation of Discharge

It is possible that the discharge is revoked in the case of fraud and refusing to obey court orders.

Reaffirmation

Reaffirmation occurs when the debtor promises to pay a debt that has been previously discharged. This is difficult to achieve in practice.

Business Reorganization—Chapter 11

Chapter 11 is an alternative to liquidation under Chapter 7. The objective is to keep the business running by allowing the debtor to keep the assets. A reorganization plan is set up. Expect to see questions on specific rules.

Debt Adjustment Plans—Chapter 13

Chapter 13 mostly applies to individuals. This section is not heavily tested but you may want to spend 5 to 10 minutes on the review to get a general idea.

The Bankruptcy Abuse Prevention and Consumer Protection Act of 2005

Major points on the amendments to the bankruptcy code:

- A large portion of vendor claims can be treated as administrative expenses that have a higher priority status.
- Payments of severance pay or retention bonuses to key employees are now limited.
- For consumer cases, a repeat of Chapter 7 or Chapter 11 discharge will be denied if the petition is made within eight (instead of six) years of the previous discharge.
- Amendments are also made to facilitate cross-border bankruptcy proceedings.

Module 31: Debtor-Creditor Relationships

This is a module with technical terms that could cause a lot of confusion to international candidates. The first part on the rights and duties of debtors and creditors requires a fair amount of memorization, but the parts on surety and guarantors are straightforward once you get familiar with the meaning of the terms. If you are confused, read the examples first, then go back and reread the concepts.

Rights and Duties of Debtors and Creditors

The module begins with an overview of the rights and duties under different scenarios. The concept of "lien" is also introduced—liens are creditors' claims on the property to secure payment or fulfill the obligations.

You may want to spend a fair amount of time studying the different types of liens and how they affect the rights and duties of debtors and creditors in each case.

Nature of Suretyship and Guaranty

This section introduces the concepts of suretyship and guaranty, how the respective agreements can be formed, and the difference between the two.

Suretyship and guaranty are two similar concepts—surety is typically primarily liable while guarantor is secondarily liable. If you are new to these terms, take the time to review the materials carefully.

Creditors' Rights and Remedies

This section goes through the rights of creditors against the principal debtor, surety, and guarantor of collection.

Surety's and Guarantor's Rights and Remedies

This is a similar discussion focusing on the rights of surety and guarantor and how they can recover their loss by various means.

Surety's and Guarantor's Defenses

In general, the surety can exercise defense that would be available to the debtor as well as his or her own. There are many examples in this section that you can review to understand the concepts.

Cosureties

Cosureties exist when there is more than one surety to the same creditor. You can expect questions on how cosureties share their liabilities and how a discharge of one cosurety may impact the rest of the cosureties. Some of these questions may be computational.

Surety Bonds

This is a brief discussion of surety bonds and related terms such as performance bonds, fidelity bonds, and official bonds. A basic understanding of these terms is sufficient for the exam.

Module 32: Agency

Agency is an important topic within business law. You can focus on the concepts of actual authority versus apparent authority and the respective responsibilities of principals and agents.

Characteristics

The module begins with the definition of agency—a relationship between two parties in which one party agrees to act on behalf of the other with respect to third parties.

One of the most common examples of agency is the employer-employee relationship. For the purpose of the CPA exam, you need to distinguish the difference between employees and independent contractors because the liability of the employer resulting from these two parties is different.

This section also goes through other examples such as power of attorney, broker, exclusive agent, del credere, e-agent, and subagent.

Methods of Creation

There are rules on the methods of creating an agency contract and when a written contract is required.

Authority

This section discusses the concept of actual authority and apparent authority. An agent has actual authority when he or she is given the power by the principal to act on the principal's behalf. An agent has apparent authority when third parties reasonably believe that they have actual authority when in fact they do not. The concept of authority is important in determining the liabilities to third parties.

Capacity to Be Agent of Principal

Principals must be able to give legal consent. Special consideration is given to minors (persons under 18 or 21 years of age) appointing an agent.

Obligations and Rights

This section focuses primarily on the duties of principals and agents. In an employer-employee agent relationship, their respective duties are based on the employment agreement.

Termination of Principal-Agent Relationship

This section goes through the consideration when terminating an agent relationship. In general, either party may terminate the agreement. Necessary steps, such as disclosure to the third party, may be required to prevent apparent authority.

Module 33: Regulation of Business Employment, Environment, and Antitrust

This module covers a long list of laws that affect employers, employees, and corporations. I encourage you to read over the review materials once and use the summary below as a reminder.

Federal Social Security Act

This Act was enacted for the social security of people in need in U.S. society. Programs covered include old age insurance, survivor's and disability insurance, hospital insurance (Medicare but not Medicaid), and unemployment insurance.

Workers' Compensation Act

The purpose of this Act is to facilitate the employees to receive compensation due to job-related injuries without the need to sue the employer. It is important to note that no fault is required to be shown. This removes the employer's common law defenses related to negligence on the part of the employee.

Employee Safety

The focus is on the Occupational Safety and Health Act (OSHA).

Employment Discrimination

Title VII of the 1964 Civil Rights Act forbids discrimination in employment on the basis of race, color, sex, or regional or national origin.

Federal Fair Labor Standards Act

All covered employees must be paid at least the minimum wage.

National Labor Relations Act

This Act provides employees the right to join, assist, or form labor organizations.

Federal Consolidated Omnibus Budget Reconciliation Act (COBRA)

If the employee quits, he or she may keep the same group health insurance coverage for 18 months for him- or herself and the spouse. The former employee is responsible for the insurance payment.

Pensions

Employee Retirement Income Security Act (ERISA) requires that the pension plan, if established, should meet certain standards.

Worker Adjustment and Retraining Notification Act

A 60-day notice must be given to employees and local and state officials in the event of plant closure or mass layoffs.

Federal Employee Polygraph Protection Act

The Act allows security services, employers who deal with national defense issues, and drug manufacturers and distributors to perform polygraph (lie detector) tests.

Employer Rights to Email

Employees generally have no expectation of privacy using an employer's email system.

Environmental Regulation

Related acts include National Environmental Policy Act, Clean Air Act, Clean Water Act, Safe Drinking Water Act, Oil Pollution Act, among many others.

Telephone Consumer Protection Act

This Act restricts telephone solicitations and the use of automated telephone equipment.

Federal Telecommunications Act

The Federal Telecommunications Act promotes competition by preventing local or state governments from blocking entry of new players in the telecommunications industry.

Identity Theft

Banks, savings associations, and credit unions are required to have an identity theft prevention program.

Antitrust Law

Antitrust laws preserve free and competitive markets.

Sherman Act of 1890

Contracts, combinations, conspiracies, or agreements in restraint of trade are illegal under this Act.

Clayton Act of 1914

The Clayton Act prohibits a corporation from acquiring the stock of a competitor to substantially lessen competition or create a monopoly.

Federal Trade Commission Act of 1914

This Act led to the establishment of the Federal Trade Commission (FTC). The FTC has the authority to enforce most of the antitrust laws but not criminal violations.

Robinson-Patman Act of 1936

This Act prohibits price discrimination, that is, when a seller charges different prices to different buyers of the same good. Price difference is permitted if there is a cost justification or is done on a temporary basis.

Module 34: Property

Property law is not covered in some review course materials. It could be a lightly tested area, but it is prudent for you to quickly read over the materials and work on the practice questions.

Distinctions between Real and Personal Property

Real property includes land and property attached to land in a permanent manner, such as a building. Personal property is property that is not real property or a fixture.

Personal Property

Personal property can be acquired as a gift, passed down under the terms of a will, or include property that is lost or abandoned. How the personal property is acquired determines the ownership, that is, the owner of its title.

Bailments

A bailment exists when an owner of personal property gives possession without giving title to another, such as giving car keys to a valet at a restaurant. This section discusses the types of bailment, bailee's duty of care, and termination of bailment.

Intellectual Property and Computer Technology Rights

This section focuses primarily on the purposes behind the intellectual property laws such as copyright law, patent law, trade secrets law, and those specifically protecting the technology sector such as the Semiconductor Chip Protection Act, Federal Counterfeit Access Device and Computer Fraud and Abuse Act, and trademarks under the Lanham Act.

Interests in Real Property

The interest in real property is listed in order to determine ownership rights in terms of present interest, future interest, and concurrent interest. There are again much legal jargon such as fee simple absolute and fee simple defeasible, but the concepts are very simple.

Contracts for Sale of Land

This section reviews the process of preparing contracts for the sale of land, including when the contract should be made and when escrows are used.

Deeds and Other Miscellaneous Topics

- **Types of deeds:** There are warranty deeds, bargain and sale deeds (grant deeds), and quitclaim deeds. You can move on as long as you can distinguish the three.
- **Executing a deed:** A deed must have the description of the real estate. There is also discussion on what it takes for the deed to become effective.
- **Recording a deed:** A process to give constructive notice to the world of grantee's ownership. There are more examples on recording a deed under different scenarios.
- **Title insurance:** Used to ensure that the title of the property is good and to cover warranties by the seller.
- **Adverse possession:** A situation where a nonowner of the land may acquire the title if he or she holds it for the statutory period. Statutory period ranges from 5 to 20 years depending on the state. The original owner must commence legal action to take back the land.
- **Easement by prescription:** A person obtains the right to use another's land (easement) in ways similar to adverse possession.
- **Mortgages:** Lien on real property to secure payment of loans.

Module 35: Individual Taxation

Individual taxation represents 13 to 19 percent of the exam content. You must know the exclusions, deductions, and exemptions inside out. It is tough because there are intense memorization tasks and calculations involved.

For international candidates who have never seen a U.S. individual tax form (Form 1040), it is helpful for you to download a copy for reference from the Internal Revenue Service website at www.irs.gov.

Gross Income on Individual Returns

Expect to memorize the following:

- Items included as gross income.
- Items excluded as gross income (known as the exclusion).
- Accounting periods (calendar year versus fiscal year).
- Tax accounting methods (cash, accrual, installment, and percentage-of-completion methods) and how they should be applied.
- Business income and deductions.
- Depreciation, depletion, and amortization.
- Domestic production activities deduction (DPAD).

In particular, for items included and excluded in gross income, you are expected to know the details down to the level of the dollar-amount thresholds.

"Above the Line" Deductions

Deductions are amounts that are subtracted from income to arrive at the adjusted gross income, also known as the *taxable income*. This is different from exclusion, which means items that are excluded from the gross income in the first place.

There are 12 types of deductions and you need to go through a similar exercise of memorizing the details.

Itemized Deductions from Adjusted Gross Income

Itemized deductions reduce the adjusted gross income and therefore are also known as *below the line* deductions (the line being the adjusted gross income).

A taxpayer has a choice to use a standard deduction or an itemized deduction to reduce the adjusted gross income. A taxpayer will therefore choose the latter only when the total itemized deduction is greater than that from the standard deduction.

For the purpose of the CPA exam, you must memorize the standard deduction, which ranges from $5,800 to $11,600 depending on the four filing statuses. There are additional standard deductions for old age and blindness.

There are also five major and a few miscellaneous deductions that you need to memorize in detail.

Exemptions

Similar to deductions, personal exemptions reduce the adjusted gross income. Personal exemptions are allowed (as a fixed amount) for taxpayer, spouse, and dependent if the dependent is a U.S. citizen or resident. You may want to refer to the review materials for the respective qualifying tests.

Tax Computation

I do not think you need to memorize the tax table but you will be required to come up with the adjusted gross income and apply the correct tax rate based on a tax table schedule. You should also know how to apply the appropriate tax rate based on filing status and whether to use the alternative minimum tax (AMT).

Note

The AMT calculation is complicated and many readers told me how they wanted to give up and ignore this topic. My suggestion is to never give up, and go through as many practice questions as possible, studying how each step is done in the calculation. Refer to my tips on mastering cost accounting calculation (another difficult topic) in Chapter 13.

Tax Credits/Estimated Tax Payments

Tax credits are used to reduce the amount of tax payable. They are:

- Applicable to target populations such as small business owners, first-time home buyers, low-income individuals, the elderly, and the disabled.
- Used to incentivize businesses and individuals on government initiatives such as energy saving and businesses providing accessibility to disabled individuals.

Filing Requirements

This is a quick discussion on how the tax filing should be made.

Farming Income and Expenses

This section goes over the tax rules specific to a farming business. I do not have statistics to back it up but I doubt if this is a heavily tested area.

Tax Procedures

This section discusses the situation where a taxpayer disagrees with the decision of the IRS. The steps are quite detailed but are generally based on common sense.

I suggest that you read through the review materials, then imagine yourself in the situation and how you would go through each step, from being audited by the IRS to reaching an agreement.

> **Note**
>
> A reader commented on his REG study experience: "Just when I think I have it down they throw in an exception or an exception to the exception to the exception. . . ." If you feel the same way, you are not alone, but you will be amazed how much you can memorize with hard work and commitment.

Module 36: Transactions in Property

This module represents 16 to 20 percent of REG exam content, certainly a section that you need to focus on in addition to individual taxation.

Sales and Other Dispositions

The module begins with a discussion on the basis of property and how this is determined by its cost, purchase price, and fair market value (FMV) upon a sale, exchange, or disposition. Candidates are required to know which basis is used under the specific fact situation.

Capital Gains and Losses

Candidates are expected to know the calculation of capital gains and losses, and how the calculation is affected by factors such as the holding period (long term versus short term). The more difficult part of this section is memorizing the exceptions and special rules, for example, in the case for corporations.

Personal Casualty and Theft Gains and Losses

This type of property is considered separately. You are expected to know the tax treatment in the case of personal casualty gain and personal casualty loss.

Gains and Losses on Business Property

Property used in business is not considered capital assets and therefore special rules apply. There is an extensive discussion on the Section 1231 properties and the depreciation recapture. Candidates should be able to determine whether the recognized gain or loss is capital, Section 1231 or ordinary, and how to apply the respective tax treatments.

Module 37: Partnership Taxation

This is a section with lots of miscellaneous details. Similar to the other taxation modules, you have to study hard and get familiar with the calculations.

Entity Classifications

The module begins with an introduction to various forms of partnerships, including general partnerships, limited partnerships, limited liability partnerships (LLP), limited liability companies (LLC), electing large partnerships, and publicly traded partnerships.

Partnership Formation

The discussion focuses on whether gain or loss is recognized in the formation of a partnership. Although as a general rule, no gain or loss is recognized when there is a contribution of property to the partnership in exchange for an interest in the partnership, there are some notable exceptions. Refer to the review materials for details.

Partnership Income and Loss

A partnership is not a separate taxpaying entity, so the income and loss from a partnership requires special treatment.

- First, items with special tax characteristics (e.g., subject to certain exclusion) are segregated and taken into account by each partner.
- Second, the remaining items are netted to arrive at the ordinary income or loss from trade or business activities.

Partnership Agreements

The proportion of income or loss for each partner is determined by the partnership agreement. This section discusses further the treatment when the property is contributed by a partner, or in the case of family partnerships.

Other Miscellaneous Topics

- **Partner's basis in partnership:** Discusses how a partner's basis is increased and decreased under different scenarios.
- **Transactions with controlled partnerships:** Special treatment is required if the transaction involves more than 50 percent of the partnership.
- **Taxable year of partnership:** A partnership must adopt the taxable year used by one or more of its partners owning an aggregate interest of more than 50 percent in profits and capital. If these partners have different year-ends, the partnership will adopt the taxable year used by all principal partners.
- **Partnership's use of cash method:** Discusses the situation when a partner can use the cash method.
- **Termination or continuation of partnership:** Goes through the tax treatment due to sale, exchange, merger and division of partnerships.
- **Sale of a partnership interest:** In most cases a capital gain or loss is recognized, but you should also be aware of the situation where ordinary gain is recognized.
- **Pro rata distributions from parternship:** No gain or loss is recognized on distribution, but gain is recognized if money received exceeds the partner's partnership basis. Loss is recognized only on complete liquidation.
- **Non–pro rata distributions from partnership:** Sometimes distribution is not done pro rata based on the partnership agreement. This section discusses the tax treatment in this special situation.

- Optional Section 754 adjustment to the basis of partnership property.
- Mandatory adjustments to basis of partnership property.

Module 38: Corporate Taxation

This could be a frustrating module because the topic is very broad, but you must master this section because it is one of the biggest and most heavily tested areas in REG.

In the CPA exam, you might see questions on income inclusion or deduction that is business-related but not individual-related. This means that you have to understand the difference between the two.

Corporations

This section focuses primarily on the tax consequences of corporation formation, variations from individual taxation, tax treatment of affiliated and controlled corporations, as well as dividends and distribution.

Comparison of C Corporations, S Corporations, and Partnerships

This section compares the three structures in terms of formation, operation, effect on owner and entity in the event of nonliquidating distribution, as well as the same effects in the event of liquidating distribution.

Multijurisdictional Taxation

There is a discussion on state and local taxation (SALT) and international taxation, including U.S. taxation of foreign persons and U.S. taxation of U.S. persons in foreign activities, and foreign tax credit.

Module 39: Other Taxation Topics

Gift and estate taxation is easier in my opinion but I do have readers who got totally stuck. The focus on REG should be first on individual taxation and corporate taxation, followed by partnership taxation, property taxation, and then these miscellaneous topics.

Gift and Estate Taxation

Gift tax is based on property transferred during an individual's lifetime, while estate tax is based on the transfer upon an individual's death. In the CPA exam, you might be asked to arrive at the taxable gifts based on the gross gift amount and various deductions. The same applies for estate tax.

Generation-Skipping Tax

The rule is designed to prevent individuals from escaping a generation of gift or estate tax. This is a flat rate at 35 percent. Refer to the review materials for a few exceptions.

Income Taxation of Estate and Trusts

While estates and trusts are separate taxable entities, there is no income tax imposed if they distribute all income to beneficiaries. This section goes over the classification of trust, computation of estate or trust taxable income, and the tax treatment on their termination.

Exempt Organizations

There are many types of exempt organizations in the United States. Special attention should be paid to Sec. 501(c)(3) organizations, which are typically religious, educational, or charitable in nature. You should have a basic understanding of which tax form is applicable for exempt organizations without the need to memorize the details in the forms.

Reader's Sharing

Finally, I share with you this story of my reader who took REG twice.

In the first exam, she got mostly tax questions in both multiple-choice and simulations. She was at such a complete loss in corporate tax that she knew she would fail before walking out. In her second attempt (two months later) she studied everything and made sure she nailed the corporate tax. In this exam, she only got three to four questions on corporate tax but many more questions on law and professional responsibilities. Lesson learned: You never know which area will be tested. You should therefore work hard to cover everything in order to pass this exam.

CHAPTER 13

Business Environment and Concepts (BEC)

BEC is the shortest and, for most candidates, least difficult to handle among the four sections. Here is the examination specification released by the American Institute of Certified Public Accountants (AICPA):

- Corporate governance (16 to 20 percent)
- Economic concepts and analysis (16 to 20 percent)
- Financial management (19 to 23 percent)
- Information systems and communications (15 to 19 percent)
- Strategic planning (10 to 14 percent)
- Operations management (12 to 16 percent)

This is a three-hour examination with three testlets each containing 30 multiple-choice questions, and one testlet containing three written communication tasks. Multiple-choice represents 80 to 90 percent of the score with written communications representing the rest. There are no task-based simulation questions in BEC.

Passing Rate History and Trend

As Figure 13.1 shows, while the passing rate was considerably better in 2012 at 52.8 percent, the long-term average is still below 50 percent. The data shows that BEC is in fact not easier to pass than the other three. Do not repeat past candidates' mistakes and underestimate the difficulty of this section.

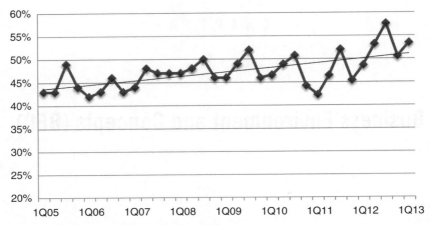

Figure 13.1   BEC Exam Passing Rate Trend, 2005–2012

Source: www.aicpa.org.

My Own Experience in BEC

I am an economics major with relevant experience in many aspects of this exam and therefore was expecting an easy time. Judging from how I did in the practices and mock exam, I was so confident that I expected a score in the 90s.

Once I started the multiple-choice section, I realized how dangerous BEC could be.

Because it is such a general topic, the examiners can surprise you with all sorts of questions. And, indeed, the questions were "odd"—it is not like they were difficult; I just was not sure I got them right.

For Financial Accounting and Reporting (FAR) and Audit and Attestations (AUD), I left the exam site knowing I nailed the exams, but no, not for BEC. I got an 87, which was pretty decent but lower than what I expected.

Study and Exam-Taking Tips

Here are some suggestions on how you can prepare for the exam effectively and efficiently.

Do Not Underestimate BEC

A few readers pass FAR, AUD, and REG on their first attempts but get stuck with BEC forever—they retake this section multiple times and still cannot get through.

If you expect BEC to be a breeze but end up struggling with it, you will lose the momentum to study and the confidence to pass. Put in the same amount of effort and commitment as you do for the other sections.

Tackle Each Topic One at a Time

BEC is a mixed bag of miscellaneous business and financial concepts. Unlike other sections such as AUD, the topics do not build on one another.

Some candidates find it difficult to retain information on topics that do not relate to each other. The solution is to tackle them one at a time—review the notes, work on the practice questions, understand the concepts, and rework the questions you did wrong. Then move on to the next topic.

It is important to stick with your study plan to avoid spending too much time on one particular topic. In case you run out of time, go straight to cost accounting (because it is tough for most people), followed by corporate governance and financial management (because they are important topics). It is worthwhile to skim through the chapter on information technology (IT) as well to get familiar with the terminology. Other tested areas in BEC are relatively straightforward and if absolutely necessary, you can guess your way through based on common sense.

Beware of Cost Accounting

Candidates tend to find cost accounting difficult to handle, because many of us do not have practical experience in manufacturing companies. There are many calculations involved, but once you understand how the computation works, you can get the correct answer every time. I show you how to master cost accounting later in the chapter.

Memorize the Formulas

For BEC you must remember the formulas (especially financial ratios) and know how to apply them in answering the questions.

Save Enough Time for Written Communication Tasks

The written communication represents 15 percent of the exam. It may sound insignificant, but if you do poorly, it will cost you the passing grade.

Most candidates will do fine if sufficient time (one hour or more) is allocated for this part of the exam. For international candidates who need more guidance on business writing, refer to Chapter 9, "How to Ace the Written Communication Tasks," for details.

Presenting the Outline

Following is the outline of the BEC exam content as well as suggestions on how to approach the review materials. The outline is written based on the *Wiley CPA Exam Review* but the tips are applicable to other review courses.

Module 40: Corporate Governance, Internal Control, and Enterprise Risk Management

Corporate governance monitors and controls professional management, and ensures that management acts in the best interest of the shareholders. Internal control is a process designed to provide reasonable assurance of reliable financial reporting, efficient and effective operation, and compliance with rules and regulations. Enterprise risk management is another process designed to manage risk within the corporation's risk appetite.

This is an important section representing 16 to 20 percent of exam content. Expect to see numerous questions on the board of directors and the audit committee, as well as internal control.

Corporate Governance

This topic focuses primarily on monitoring roles of the stakeholders:

- Internal: Board of directors and internal auditors.
- External: External auditors, analysts, credit agencies, attorneys, the SEC, and the IRS.

The concept of corporate governance should be familiar to accountants with different backgrounds and I suggest spending no more than 15 minutes on the review but allocate lots of time to the practice questions. For international candidates, you may want to read the section on the board of directors more carefully because the U.S. board structure may be different from the one used in your country.

Internal Controls

The internal control framework developed by the Committee of Sponsoring Organizations (COSO) is the most common and is the one tested on the CPA exam. Memorize the following five components of internal control and understand each of the functions:

1. The control environment
2. Risk assessment process
3. Control activities
4. Information and communication
5. Monitoring

It is also important to know that there are limitations of internal control and you are expected to understand the details of these limitations.

Internal control is an important topic throughout the CPA exam. Related discussions can be found in Module 41, "Information Technology," later in this chapter and Module 3, "Understanding Internal Control and Assessing Control Risk," in Chapter 10.

Note

Many CPA review courses create mnemonics for the components of internal control. You may want to find your own creative ways to help with the memorization.

Enterprise Risk Management

Enterprise risk management (ERM) is another framework developed by COSO. Similarly, find a creative way to memorize and understand the eight components of ERM:

1. Internal environment
2. Objective setting
3. Event identification
4. Risk assessment
5. Risk response
6. Control activities
7. Information and communication
8. Monitoring

You can see this as a similar concept that is applied to how companies manage their risks.

Note

Some CPA review materials have overly extensive coverage on corporate governance in my opinion. Be careful with time management here—if you plan to complete the BEC study within one to two months, you should not dwell on this topic for more than a week.

Module 41: Information Technology

Information technology (IT) is such a big topic that none of the CPA review course can cover it all. It is understandable if you feel underprepared in this section, but the good news is that most candidates are in the same situation. Take the time to go over the basic terminology, think through how IT can impact an auditor's work, and move on to the practice questions.

IT represents 15 to 19 percent of content in this section. The auditing procedure related to IT is tested in AUD.

Information Systems within a Business

This is an overview of information systems and how they are designed for a business environment. If you work in corporate accounting, this is common sense but if you are a fresh graduate or work in a completely different field then you may want to take longer to read through this section.

Characteristics of Computer Systems—General

This section is meant to be a general overview of the following components in an information system:

- Types of computers, hardware, and software.
- Methods of processing.
- Methods of data structure (data organization and file structure).

Note

There are numerous terms in this section. You can never memorize all of them. Instead, focus on understanding what the terms mean and how they relate to one another.

Characteristics of Computer Systems—Specific

This is a more in-depth discussion on specific parts of a computer system, such as the network, microcomputers, end-user computing, and electronic commerce. More important, you are expected to understand the control implication for each component of the system.

Control Objectives for Information and Related Technology (COBIT)

COBIT is a framework for integrating IT with business strategy. Go over the specific IT resources used to achieve this objective.

Effect of IT on Internal Control

This section echoes the discussion on control implications of computer systems but the ideas are presented from the auditor's perspective. Key areas include:

- Overall principles of a reliable system and overall risks.
- How IT affects the factors of the five components of internal control.
- Computer general control activities.
- Computer application control activities.
- Disaster recovery and business continuity plans.

Flowcharting

It is helpful to go through a list of common flowchart symbols in case they appear in multiple-choice or task-based simulation questions.

Note

A reader once told me that studying IT is like reading how a car works without ever seeing a car. I cannot agree with him more.

IT can look intimidating at first, but the topics are mostly factual. As long as you go through the terms and try your best to understand what they mean, especially in the context of how they affect the internal control, you will do fine and can move on to the next topic.

Module 42: Economics, Strategy, and Globalization

Economics is all about explaining everyday life in a scientific way. If you have never taken a class in this subject, it is worth the time to go through the terminology, charts, and graphs. They are easy points to score once you understand the underlying concepts.

This module also touches on how globalization impacts location economies and the shift in economic power between developing and developed countries.

Microeconomics

This is an introduction to microeconomics covering key concepts:

- Demand, demand curve shift, and elasticity
- Supply, supply curve shift, and elasticity
- Market equilibrium
- Fixed cost, variable cost, and other costs of production
- Relationship between marginal revenue and marginal cost

Note

Some readers get completely stuck with this topic because they have a hard time understanding the graphs. If you are in the same situation, you may want to borrow an introduction to microeconomics textbook and read the first few chapters. The concepts should be easy to comprehend with more explanations and examples.

Macroeconomics

Macroeconomics looks at the economy in big picture. Key concepts include:

- Common terms such as GDP, GNP, and real versus nominal GDP.
- Aggregate demand and supply, interest rate effect, and wealth effect.
- Business cycles (and the related graphs).
- Impact of investment on the economy.
- Unemployment, inflation, and the causal relationship between them.
- Various monetary policies and their uses.
- Fiscal policies such as taxes.
- Global economy and the concepts of absolute advantage versus comparative advantage, obstacles to free trade, and related organizations such as WTO, NAFTA, IMF, G-20, and EU.
- Foreign exchange rates and the influencing factors.
- Foreign investments.

Note

This section is longer than microeconomics and the large number of subtopics may look overwhelming. Take the time to go over the terms carefully and think about how they relate to major economic events you see on the news every day. Once you make the relationship, you will be able to answer these questions with common sense.

Effects of the Global Economic Environment on Strategy

This is a section that summarizes the impact of globalization and how the comparative advantages in each country may affect the strategy of businesses.

In my opinion, this is one of the easiest and more interesting topics. You should not spend more than 15 minutes reading through this section.

> **Note**
>
> Accounting and finance professionals with international backgrounds should have no problem tackling this part of the exam, but non-U.S. candidates should be aware that the questions are written in the United States (i.e., developed market) perspective, which might be different from yours if you live and work in an emerging market.

Module 43: Financial Risk Management and Capital Budgeting

This module focuses on the balance of risk and return. Management aims to maximize return based on a company's risk appetite. There is also a discussion on how to mitigate risk by using techniques such as hedging and diversification.

The concept of present value is also important in this module and in BEC in general. You are expected to know the common applications, such as the valuation of bonds.

Risk and Return

Risk and return are the basic concepts for investment and financial decision making. In this section, candidates are required to calculate the expected return for a single asset and a portfolio. You also need to know the impact of interest rates on risk. You will do well as long as you understand the relationships of the key terms (risk, return, and interest rate) and the formulas for their calculation.

Derivatives and Hedging

There are many technical terms in this section such as options, forwards, futures, and swaps. If you have not studied derivatives before, this could be daunting to read and to understand how each of them works. The best way to master the concepts is to learn through an example or by working on a few practice questions to see how the concepts are applied.

Present Value

Candidates should know the calculation of present value (PV) and future value (FV), which you can easily master by doing lots of practice questions. The tougher part in this section is how this concept is applied to the valuation of bonds. You may want to review the relevant section on bonds in FAR for a complete picture.

Capital Budgeting

Management makes use of capital budgeting to evaluate investment projects. It is important to memorize the basic formulas for these methodologies for the exam:

- Payback and discounted payback
- Accounting rate of return (ARR)
- Net present value (NPV)
- Internal rate of return (IRR)

You should know how to estimate the risk of investment projects using the following methodologies:

- Probability analysis
- Risk-adjusted discounted rate
- Time-adjusted discount rates
- Sensitivity analysis
- Scenario analysis
- Decision trees
- Real options
- The decision of lease versus buy
- Portfolio risk

There are calculations involved in applying these methodologies but there may not be formulas to remember. The best way to get prepared is to work on as many practice questions as possible to cover most if not all of these methodologies.

Note

For candidates who have not taken a related finance class or worked on financial modeling before, this could be a challenging module. The trick is to truly understand how the calculation works using the basic formulas. If you do not understand the calculation flow, ask the instructor in your class, or contact your instructor or counselor if you get a self-study review course.

Module 44: Financial Management

This module focuses primarily on how management makes financial decisions based on various tools and analyses.

This is a heavily tested topic representing 19 to 23 percent of exam content. You will see a mixture of conceptual and computational questions. The good news is that the materials are relatively straightforward especially if you have some background in finance.

Working Capital Management

This section deals with the management of current assets and current liabilities. For most companies, working capital management focuses on inventories and receivables. You need to understand how the inventory and receivable conversion periods are calculated using the formulas.

For cash management, the goal is to minimize cash on hand while having a sufficient amount for ad hoc needs. Other related concepts include management of marketable securities, financing short-term assets, and sourcing short-term funds and loans. Management may use multiple methods to maintain the optimal level.

Capital Structure

This section covers long-term debt and equity, and how management balances the weight of debt and equity to achieve the optimal capital structure for the company.

Debt The first step is to understand the various types of bonds and understand the differences between them. The second step is to think through debt in a macro perspective, such as the advantages and disadvantages of bond financing, and how debt in general can be repaid.

There are some calculations in this section, mostly on bond yields. You can also refer to the section on Present Value under Module 43, "Financial Risk Management and Capital Budgeting," for more discussion on bond valuation.

Equity Similarly, take the time to understand the terms and the differences between each type of equity.

Evaluate the Best Source of Financing   The evaluation requires that you have a good knowledge of debt and equity. For example, there is a fair amount of calculation involved in Capital Asset Pricing Model (CAPM) and arbitrage pricing model, which are almost impossible to solve unless you understand the cost of debt versus cost of equity. This section also covers dividends and share repurchases. These topics are relatively straightforward.

Asset and Liability Valuation

Asset and liability valuation provide important information for financial decision making. You can spend 5 to 10 minutes reading on the types of valuation models and which model is appropriate for each scenario.

Mergers

This should be another quick read. You may want to get familiar with key terms such as synergies, goodwill, and fair value, then spend five minutes reading about the rationale behind a merger, and how firms are evaluated using discounted cash flow (DCF) analysis and the market multiple method.

Module 45: Performance Measures

This module discusses how management measures financial and nonfinancial performance in the organization. While there may be technical terms such as *balanced score cards*, *value chain*, and *benchmarking*, candidates can usually get the correct answers using common sense. I encourage spending no more than 30 minutes reviewing the material, then go straight to the practice questions.

Note

Performance measures may involve calculation using profitability ratios. You can get a list of common ratios here: http://ipassthecpaexam.com/cpa-exam-financial-ratios/.

Module 46: Cost Measurement

This module focuses on how the costs of a product can be allocated to each production unit. The following cost systems are discussed:

- Job-order costing
- Process costing
- Activity-based costing

Candidates should know how to perform a full calculation and how to use journal entries to show the flow of cost items between the financial statements.

Cost accounting is the most challenging section in BEC for most candidates. The concepts seem to be intuitive but once you work on the question, you get all the answers wrong. I struggled with cost accounting myself and I know how frustrating this can be for many candidates. But once you make yourself sit down and understand the reasons behind the formulas, it is not that bad . . . in fact, once it clicks, you can get the correct answer every time. Here is how I overcome my fear in cost accounting.

How to Master Cost-Accounting Calculations

Assuming you have a home-study DVD, this is what you can do:

- Watch the video.
- Stop when there is a practice problem.
- Have pen and paper ready. Follow the instructor and write down every step—do not just go through the steps in your head.

Try your best to understand the concept; if not, go back to the first step.

- Test yourself by doing the same problem on your own. Show all the steps in writing.
- Check your answer. Because you wrote everything down, it should be easy to realize if you miss any steps.
- Most of you should get the "click" by now. If you still do not get it, call or email your instructor.

You can also go through a similar exercise using any CPA exam review books.

Cost of Goods Manufactured

This is an overview of the cost of goods manufactured (CGM). You are expected to understand the flow of a CGM statement and how CGM is related to the cost of goods sold.

Cost Flows

It is important to understand how cost items flow on the balance sheet and income statement. You may want to come back and analyze the journal entries again after reading through the entire module.

Job-Order Costing

Job-order costing is one of the costing systems. You are expected to understand the flow of each cost item and how to fill in the job cost sheets. The best way to master job-order costing and other cost systems is to go through the calculation step by step and rework the steps until you understand the underlying concepts and the flow.

Accounting for Overhead

In this section, you might be asked to account for overhead items in the form of fixed and variable overhead costs.

Disposition of Under- and Overapplied Overhead

The under- or overapplied overhead is typically written off to the cost of goods sold.

Service Department Cost Allocation

Service departments are support functions the cost of which benefits multiple production departments. The cost is allocated based on direct method, step method, and reciprocal method. Go through each of these allocation methods in the review materials.

Process Costing

Process costing is another type of costing system. Unlike job-order costing, this system is more suitable for production involving a continuous process (such as oil refining). Each processing department is considered a cost center. Similar to job-order costing, you should be able to understand the concepts in order to perform a full calculation.

Hybrid-Costing System

The hybrid-costing system is used when manufacturers combine the job-costing and process systems. This is applicable to industries such as car manufacturing and clothes manufacturing.

Backflush Costing

Backflush costing uses standard costs to work backward to "flush out" the costs of goods finished or sold. This costing method is commonly used in a just-in-time production system.

Activity-Based Costing

Activity-based costing is the third costing system covered in this module. Similar to joint-based and process costing, candidates should understand the underlying concepts and be able to perform full calculations.

Joint Products

In this section you need to understand the joint costs incurred from the joint products and how this common cost can be allocated.

By-Products

By-products are products created "on the side" with little marketable value. They are either recognized as a reduction of production cost or as ordinary sales or other income.

Estimating Cost Functions

A cost function is a mathematical expression that represents the relationship between a level of activity and the resulting cost. The concept is much clearer if presented in graphical form. Candidates are expected to be familiar with methodologies such as scattergraph, high-low method, regression analysis, and correlation analysis, but you are not required to perform a full calculation.

Module 47: Planning, Control, and Analysis

This is another module that involves calculations in the break-even analysis and costing. Although it is generally not as tough as

Module 46, you should allocate sufficient time to get a good understanding of both the concepts and the computations.

Note

It is interesting to note that candidates find cost accounting either very difficult or very easy. I believe it depends on whether you have gotten over the hump and understand how the calculations work. Once you do, they are straightforward because the examiners are testing BEC topics at the introductory level.

Cost-Volume-Profit (CVP) Analysis

CVP analysis is also known as the *breakeven analysis.* You are expected to calculate the breakeven point (or the number of units at the breakeven point) using the fixed and variable costs.

Variable (Direct) and Absorption (Full) Costing

This is a topic that confuses many candidates but is frequently asked on the exam. It is important that you differentiate the two costing methods. Absorption costing, which is the financial treatment under generally accepted accounting principles (GAAP), does not differentiate the fixed and variable cost. Variable costing is not a GAAP treatment but is sometimes preferred in internal reporting because the separation of fixed and variable cost facilitates monitoring and decision making. It is also important to understand how the two methods may impact the financial statement, particularly on net income.

Financial Planning

Financial planning is a process of making financial projections based on a current financial statement and assumptions about future conditions. This exercise should tie in with the overall strategic plans of management. This plan can be used in budgeting and scenario analysis.

Budgeting

This is an overview of budgeting, including the types of budgets and how the budget is prepared (top-down approach, bottom-up approach, or a combination).

Forecasting Methods

This section focuses on the various forecasting methods. The discussion is very conceptual—if you get confused, it would be helpful to study one example in detail or by working through a few practice questions.

Flexible Budgets

Flexible budgets are typically used in the planning stage where the budget can be adjusted based on the change in units (e.g., number of labor hours). This can be used in scenario analysis or for management to compare actual results.

Responsibility Accounting

Responsibility accounting is a way in which managers can be held accountable based on their responsibilities. For example, the area of responsibility for a support function is a cost center, and that, with both revenue and cost target, is a profit center.

Segmented Reporting and Controllability

This section briefly discusses the ways to break down variable and absorption costing reports into smaller segments.

Standards and Variances

This is a discussion on the use of variance as well as specific terms such as *material variance, labor variance,* and *overhead variance.*

Project Management

This section focuses on the stages of project management from project initiation, planning, and execution to closure, as well as the techniques used to schedule and monitor a project.

Product and Service Pricing

This section focuses on how management sets pricing for products and services after taking into account many factors, including sales volume, customers' reactions, competitors' reactions, economic conditions, and other external factors. The relevant terms such as *cost-plus pricing* and *target pricing* are also introduced.

Transfer Pricing

Transfer pricing is a type of internal pricing where the selling sub-unit charges a certain price to a buying subunit. In this case, the costing is properly accounted for at the business unit level but is canceled out at the top level.

Short-Term Differential Cost Analysis

Finally, a discussion on differential cost decisions that may include:

- Sell or process further
- Special orders
- Outsourcing
- Closing a department or segment
- Sale of obsolete inventory
- Scarce resources

Reader's Sharing

Here are the experiences of a reader who took BEC as the last section of the CPA exam. As a person with no U.S. background, he felt disadvantaged in REG because the U.S. tax rules were like a foreign language to him. For BEC, he felt much better: Every candidate starts off with a level playing field because business concepts are similarly applied around the world.

On the BEC exam, he tried to complete the multiple-choice questions as quickly as he could to save more time for the written communication tasks, which was his weaker area. One of the writings required a good knowledge of several financial accounting concepts. Although he knew he was tested more on writing ability than technical knowledge, he was glad that he still remembered the core concepts he learned in FAR. He did pass BEC in his first attempt.

What If I Fail?

In every CPA exam, roughly half of the candidates pass while the other half do not. Failing the exam is a real possibility. It is important to discuss how you can overcome the disappointment, face the challenge again with more confidence, and successfully pass the exam on your next attempt.

Perform a Self-Evaluation

A self-evaluation is crucial to find out why you did not pass. When you calm down and have 30 minutes to spare, start going through the following.

Did You Allocate Sufficient Time to Study?

Many candidates fail simply because they did not complete the review. There could be many reasons:

- Not having a study plan.
- Not sticking to the study plan.
- Study plan not being realistic and workable.
- Underestimating the time required for review.
- Emergencies came up.

Issues with Study Plans Study plans are critical for time management throughout the study. If you failed the exam and did not have a plan, this could be the main culprit. The good thing is that you can easily improve the situation with a good plan in place on your next attempt.

If you had a plan but you consistently fell behind schedule—was the schedule being unrealistic, or was it too restrictive? Adjust the schedule to allow more time or flexibility. As a retaker, you will likely study most if not all the review materials—less time should be allocated to studying but more time to practicing.

How to Deal with Emergencies   First of all, overtime during the audit season and your sister's wedding are not emergencies. These ad hoc but expected family and work commitments should have been factored into your study plan.

Emergencies are sudden and uncontrollable events that require your immediate attention, such as the passing away of a close relative, sudden illness, or your spouse being laid off and you having to work extra to compensate for the loss of income.

With the buffer weeks included in your plan, you might be able to catch up after taking care of the incident. You may also contact the state board for the possibility of postponing the test date if you have evidence of an extreme circumstance.

Did You Put in Enough Effort?

This is a question that only you can answer. Be true to yourself and ask whether you have been putting the CPA exam as a top priority, and whether you have made sacrifices to create extra time and energy for studying.

Even if you allocated the time, have you been concentrating? During the time when you were supposed to work on the test preparation software, did you spend a good part of the time chatting on Facebook? I understand that checking email has become a necessary part of daily life. You can try setting an alarm clock to allow 10 minutes to open the most critical email. You can go through the rest after studying or when you take a break (remember to set the alarm clock for the break, too). Both the quantity and quality of study time is important for the success of your exam.

Did You Study Using Effective Review Materials?

Many candidates blame the review materials when they fail the exam. In most cases, it is a combination of many factors. Make sure that you do not jump into buying another course without completing this self-evaluation process.

If you did not get any review materials and relied only on sample questions on the American Institute of Certified Public Accountants (AICPA) website or free exam questions on the Internet, chances are that you can substantially increase your chance of success with a reputable review course.

You can refer to our discussion on CPA review courses in Chapter 7, "Study Tips and Exam-Taking Strategies," and the pros and cons comparison of major CPA review providers on my website.

Did You Work on Practice Questions?

We discussed in Chapter 7 the importance of test preparation software as both a practice tool and learning resource. If you have been reading the books, taking a class, or watching a video without actually working on the practice questions, this is definitely something you can do this time to pass the exam.

How you work on the practice questions can make a difference as well. Reading the explanation of the correct answers will help crystallize the concept and ensure that you got the correct answer for the right reason. If the answer is incorrect, it is more important for you to go through the explanations and learn how the concept should be applied, or work on the calculations until you understand how to tackle a similar question.

A reader told me that she only had three weeks to prepare for Regulation (REG). She reviewed all the study materials, did not complete the practice questions, and scored a 63. The diagnostic report revealed that the areas where she underperformed were the ones skipped in the test preparation software. She kept thinking that if she had worked on all the questions, she would have scored the required 75.

Did You Fail to Perform on Exam Day?

You may have done your best in preparing for the exam; yet on the exam day, your mind went blank. Your head was aching, your palms were sweating, and you just wanted to run out of the room and give up.

Confidence is the key to success. You gain confidence by understanding all the tested areas in the exam, but there are many other factors.

Minimizing the Uncertainties   This includes anything from knowing how to use the tools on the screen, (the flag buttons, calculator, and search functions) to visiting the test site a few days before to get an expectation of traveling time and site environment. Remove as many uncertainties as you can to reduce the stress.

Support from Family and Friends   Getting the support of family and friends is important. The fact that you know your loved ones are behind you can be a big confidence booster. If you cannot find anyone who understands your situation and gives you support, you are most welcome to join our community in the CPA exam forum.

Healthy Mind and Body   This is cliché advice, but you do need a good night's sleep for this exam. Find other ways to relax your mind and body, such as yoga, jogging in a nearby park, or watching a little bit of TV. For international candidates, it is worth arriving a few days before the exam to minimize jet lag.

Remember, the task-based simulation represents 40 percent of the total score for Financial Accounting and Reporting (FAR), Audit and Attestation (AUD), and Regulation (REG). These are questions that you cannot prepare for, but instead you must think on your feet and apply what you learned to answer the questions. A physically fit mind and body can help you achieve your very best.

Review the Diagnostic Report

Candidates who fail to pass will receive a diagnostic report that shows the relative performance in each of the tested areas.

For each of the content areas, there is an indication of "stronger," "comparable," or "weaker" so you can find out your strengths and weaknesses. There is also a similar table showing the relative performance in multiple-choice, task-based simulations, or written communication tasks.

If you failed more than once, take the time to compare the reports. The weakest areas can be identified immediately if you have a consistently lower performance in certain content areas. If there is no obvious trend, you may need to revamp the overall study strategies instead.

Recharge and Get Back the Momentum

First of all, take a well-deserved break. Then, thank your family and friends for their support. They are equally devastated when they realize things will take longer to get back to normal. You can combine the two by spending a fun day together.

But the break has to be short or you will lose the momentum or forget the materials. Complete the self-evaluation and find out how you can improve, followed by creating a detailed to-do list so you can stick with your plan.

Should I Switch and Take Another Section First?

This is the last thing you want to do, in my opinion. Unless there is a strong reason (and I cannot think of any), you should stick with the same section and get it out of the way before moving on. Here are the reasons.

You Do Not Want to Relearn the Materials Most candidates should have at least partially prepared for the exam before entering the exam room. Switching to another section would mean throwing away weeks if not months of hard work.

Switching Makes You Feel Like Giving Up This "given up" feeling will haunt you throughout the rest of your CPA journey until you eventually beat the beast. It is a negative energy that will affect your study in other sections as well.

You Have to Take It Sooner or Later There is no use in procrastinating because you must retake this section in order to get the CPA qualification.

The CPA Exam Is Not Rocket Science

A reader told me how he was overjoyed with tears after passing the exam. It had been his fifth or sixth attempt . . . I lost count. When he was finally done, all the sleepless nights and stomachaches were gone, and it was a great relief for the entire family. His children used to ask him if he passed or failed every time he took the exam and it was embarrassing to tell them the fact. He is a proud CPA now and I am so happy for him.

I admire people who finish in their first try, but I have the most respect for those who failed once, twice, or even more but eventually reached the finish line. I was once told that fewer than 20 percent of candidates pass the CPA exam on their first attempt, but 75 percent of candidates manage to complete all four sections.

Seven to eight out of 10 who tried can become a CPA. This is an encouraging statistic. Don't give up!

15

Final Words

If you have read the book up to this point, you are all ready for a successful CPA journey. Now that you have learned how to plan, study for, and pass the CPA exam, all you need to do is to . . .

Put Them in Action

Reading about the tactics is one thing, acting on them is another. Do yourself a favor and implement these strategies.

Come Back for Tips

You do not need to remember every single idea in this book. Circle, highlight, and bookmark the important pages so you can come back whenever you are ready.

Don't Be Afraid to Ask for Help

There is absolutely no reason why you should not ask for help. Your instructor, counselor, and peers are happy to help people out.

I welcome questions that you may have on this book or on the CPA exam in general. You can contact me via:

- Forum: http://forum.ipassthecpaexam.com
- Facebook: www.facebook.com/ipassthecpaexam
- Website: http://ipassthecpaexam.com

Supplementary information to this book can be downloaded for free at http://ipassthecpaexam.com/tools/.

Believe in Yourself

When the inevitable time comes when you feel so frustrated and want to give up, remember this:

> If we did all the things we were capable of doing, we would literally astound ourselves.
>
> —Thomas Edison

Believe in yourself. You can do it!

Appendix A: Countdown Plans

Check off the items from the list when you complete each of the tasks.

After Getting Your NTS

- ☐ Budget your CPA exam expenses.
- ☐ Schedule your exam sections.
- ☐ Arrange air tickets/transportation.
- ☐ Reserve hotel room.
- ☐ Apply for visa (if applicable).
- ☐ Check your primary identification.
- ☐ Check your secondary identification.
- ☐ Create or download a study plan.
- ☐ Settle on the CPA review materials.
- ☐ Start studying!

One Month before the Exam

- ☐ Double-check the name/signature on NTS, primary, and secondary IDs.
- ☐ Double-check travel and accommodation arrangements.
- ☐ Finish up studying.
- ☐ Review weaker areas.
- ☐ Decide whether to switch to "cram" mode.
- ☐ Review the availability of items that you need to bring on the trip.

One Week before the Exam

- ☐ Review the weakest areas.
- ☐ Rework practice questions you did wrong previously.
- ☐ Start packing for the trip.
- ☐ If you are to travel to the United States, check local weather conditions in advance.

One Day before the Exam

- ☐ Visit the test center if you haven't already.
- ☐ Check tomorrow's weather conditions.
- ☐ If you are driving, check whether gas tank is full.
- ☐ Final review of the critical and heavily tested areas.
- ☐ Do something relaxing.
- ☐ Sleep early.
- ☐ Tell yourself you are ready!

Appendix B: Packing for the Exam Trip

Here is a list of suggested items to bring for your exam trip if you need to stay overnight at a hotel. Check them off as you pack.

Items to Bring to the Prometric Center

- ☐ NTS
- ☐ Primary ID
- ☐ Secondary ID
- ☐ Wallet
- ☐ Mobile phone
- ☐ Jacket
- ☐ Ear plugs with no string attached (optional)
- ☐ Flash cards or final review notes
- ☐ Umbrella
- ☐ Aspirin or pain reliever
- ☐ Medications if necessary
- ☐ Small water bottle
- ☐ Snacks

Items to Bring for the Trip

- ☐ Few sets of comfortable clothes
- ☐ Underwear and socks
- ☐ Extra pair of shoes
- ☐ Extra pair of glasses

- ☐ Pajamas
- ☐ Moisturizer and lip balm
- ☐ Razor
- ☐ Mobile phone charger
- ☐ Bathing suit and goggles
- ☐ Alarm clock—do not rely only on the hotel wake-up call
- ☐ Laptop—if you choose to work on the test prep software

If you stay in a budget hotel:

- ☐ Slippers
- ☐ Soap and shampoo
- ☐ Toothbrush and toothpaste

For international candidates:

- ☐ Passport
- ☐ Phone number of local embassy for emergency assistance
- ☐ U.S. dollars
- ☐ Camera and charger
- ☐ Travel plug adapter (110V is used in the United States)

Glossary

150-Hour Rule The standard rule within the CPA exam educational requirements: Candidates are required to accumulate 150 credit hours or more from a regionally accredited educational institution to be qualified for the exam.

AICPA The professional body for CPAs in the United States. Also known as the American Institute of Certified Public Accountants.

associate degrees Undergraduate degrees granted by community colleges, junior colleges, and technical colleges. The number of years spent to complete the degree is typically two years. Three-year bachelor's degrees from non-U.S. educational institutions are considered an associate degree by the state boards.

AUD Acronym for Auditing and Attestation, one of the four exam sections of the Uniform CPA Examination.

BEC Acronym for Business Environments and Concepts, one of the four exam sections of the Uniform CPA Examination.

CBT Acronym for computer-based testing, the current CPA exam testing format. The CPA exam converted to a computer-based format in April 2004, and a new format (e-CBT) was introduced in January 2011.

community colleges Public educational institutions that provide two years of higher education. Graduates are granted an associate degree. These graduates may transfer their credits to a four-year university, complete the rest of the coursework there, and obtain a four-year bachelor's degree.

correspondence courses A type of long-distance course in which students do not attend the course in a traditional classroom setting. Correspondence courses offered by nonregional accredited educational institutions may not be counted toward the CPA exam educational requirements.

FAR   Acronym for Financial Accounting and Reporting, one of the four exam sections of the Uniform CPA Examination.

IQEX   Acronym for International Qualification Exam, a shorter version of the Uniform CPA Examination designed for candidates who are members of non-U.S. professional associations that have entered into mutual recognition agreements (MRA) with representatives of the U.S. state boards of accountancy. The content and format is equivalent to the REG exam section of the Uniform CPA Exam.

MCQ   Abbreviation of multiple-choice question.

mnemonics   A learning technique that helps in retention.

NASBA   A national association for the state boards of accountancy. NASBA is one of the CPA exam's administrators, together with the AICPA and Prometric. Also known as the National Association of State Boards of Accountancy.

nonpublic accounting   Accounting experience gained from the corporate sector instead of the professional public accounting (auditing) firms. Also known as private accounting or corporate accounting.

NTS   Acronym for Notice to Schedule. Once you are approved by the state board to sit for the exam, they mail, fax, or email you a slip known as the NTS. You can schedule the exam at one of the Prometric testing centers after obtaining your NTS. The NTS must be taken to the testing center on the day of testing.

pretest items   Not all questions on the CPA exams count toward the final score. Some are included for the development and testing for future exams. These questions are known as the *pretest items* and can appear in multiple-choice questions, task-based simulations, and written communication tasks.

Prometric   A company that operates national testing centers where you take computerized standardized tests, including the Uniform CPA Examination. There are typically several Prometric centers in each U.S. state or countries outside the United States.

public accounting   Experience gained from professional public accounting (auditing) firms.

REG   Abbreviation for Regulation, one of the four exam sections of the Uniform CPA Examination.

simulations   See **task-based simulations**.

Social Security Number   A nine-digit number issued to U.S. citizens, permanent residents, and temporary workers in order to track these individuals for social security purposes. The CPA profession is regulated and most state boards make use of SSNs to regulate their licensees.

State Board of Accountancy (State Board)   Each state's or U.S. territory's board of accountancy, which is responsible for regulating certified public accountants and related professions within their jurisdictions. All CPA licenses are granted by the 54 state boards of accountancy in the United States.

state societies of CPAs   These societies serve the professional needs of the CPA, educate the public about the profession, and encourage students to study accounting to become CPAs. There is one society of CPA in each U.S. jurisdiction.

task-based simulations (TBS)   Condensed case studies that test accounting knowledge and skills using real-life work-related situations. TBS questions represent 40 percent of the total score in FAR, AUD, and REG.

testing window   The period that the CPA exam is available, which is up to five to six days a week during the first two months of every calendar quarter throughout the year.

testlet   Technical term used in the context of the CPA exam. There are four testlets in each section of the exam: three testlets of multiple-choice questions and one testlet of task-based simulations or written communications.

upper-division   Courses that are taken in the junior or senior years (i.e., third and fourth years in the university), which are typically intermediate or advanced courses.

Acknowledgments

I am blessed by the many extraordinary people I met throughout my schooling and my career. I am especially grateful to Professor Richard Taub, then Department Head of Public Policy Studies during the time when I studied at the University of Chicago. With his encouragement, I took a graduate-level class in my second year of college. English was not my first language, but I volunteered to present my paper in a lecture hall full of graduate students. This experience tells me that the sky is the limit if I am willing to try my best.

I am also deeply thankful to Edward Lam, my supervisor at Morgan Stanley, who taught me the true meaning of hard work and how a foreigner could defy the glass ceiling and excel in one of the most competitive U.S. investment banks, then go on to become the CFO of an FT Global 500 company.

Susanna Hui, my supervisor and CFO of PCCW, was the one who encouraged me to take the CPA exam. This book would not exist without her. She has been an exemplary role model of how female finance professionals can balance family and work with grace.

I offer my thanks to the many people who have shared their expertise and experience to make this book a reality. My gratitude to Peter Milburn for discovering my website, Nick Melchior for recommending that I write this book, and the John Wiley & Sons editing team for their guidance and support; to Leslie-Anne Rogers for her expertise in the CPA exam qualification process; and to Yan, Edgar, Donna, Ying, Rania, Shilpi, and Lori for sharing their amazing stories with me, and now with all of you.

I save for last the ones to whom I owe the most: my family. My parents and sister have been the biggest cheerleaders no matter which path I have chosen, and I am glad that this latest project of mine has made them proud. My children, Megan and Max, bring much joy, happiness, and inspiration to me every day. The love and support of my husband has been unconditional. Without him, I could never pursue my dream of running my own website and becoming an author.

About the Author

Stephanie Ng graduated from the University of Chicago with a bachelor's degree in economics and is a CPA (not in public practice). She began her career as an investment banker at Lehman Brothers and Morgan Stanley before joining her clients in the finance department, where she specialized in corporate finance, mergers and acquisitions, and debt refinancing.

Stephanie launched a CPA exam preparation website, IPassTheCPAExam.com, in January 2010 to help accountants around the world obtain the U.S. CPA qualification, providing information on exam requirements, review course comparison, and exam-taking strategies. She welcomes readers' questions through her Facebook page at www.facebook.com/ipassthecpaexam.

Index

236